Understanding
YOUR
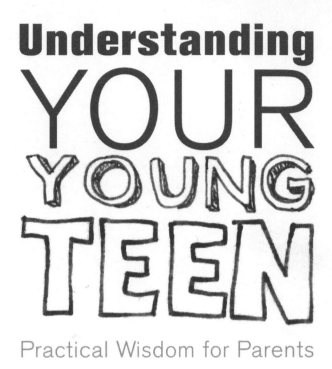
YOUNG
TEEN

Practical Wisdom for Parents

MARK OESTREICHER

Understanding
YOUR
YOUNG
TEEN

Practical Wisdom for Parents

ZONDERVAN®

ZONDERVAN.com/
AUTHORTRACKER
follow your favorite authors

ZONDERVAN

Understanding Your Young Teen: Practical Wisdom for Parents
Copyright © 2011 by Mark Oestreicher

This title is also available as a Zondervan ebook.
Visit www.zondervan.com/ebooks.

This title is also available in a Zondervan audio edition.
Visit www.zondervan.fm.

Requests for information should be addressed to:

Zondervan, *Grand Rapids, Michigan 49530*

Library of Congress Cataloging-in-Publication Data

Oestreicher, Mark.
     Understanding your young teen / Mark Oestreicher.
       p.   cm.
     Includes bibliographical references (p.   ) and index.
     ISBN 978-0-310-67114-5 (softcover : alk. paper) 1. Parent and teenager—Religious
     aspects—Christianity. 2. Parenting—Religious apects—Christianity. 3. Middle
     school students—Religious life. I. Title.
    BV4529.O345 2011
    248.8'45—dc23   2011033292

Any Internet addresses (websites, blogs, etc.) and telephone numbers in this book are offered as a resource. They are not intended in any way to be or imply an endorsement by Zondervan, nor does Zondervan vouch for the content of these sites and numbers for the life of this book.

Cover design: SharpSeven Design
Interior design: David Conn

Printed in the United States of America

11 12 13 14 15 16 /DCI/ 22 21 20 19 18 17 16 15 14 13 12 11 10 9 8 7 6 5 4 3 2 1

Contents

For Max, currently my favorite young teen

Acknowledgments

Big thanks, first of all, go out to my good friend Scott Rubin, the junior high pastor at Willow Creek Community Church. Scott and I co-authored the book *Middle School Ministry*, and he was gracious enough to allow me to re-purpose my chapters from that book for this work. Thanks also to Kurt Johnston of Saddleback Church, who worked with me almost a decade ago to create the outline for *Middle School Ministry*.

Thanks also to my friends and peers from the Junior High Pastors Summit, many of whom contributed sidebars to this book; and to Kara Powell and Brad Griffin, for their insightful and gracious contribution.

Thanks to the few, the proud, the remaining Youth Specialties publishing staff—particularly Jay Howver and Roni Meek—who were still willing to publish this book even when they no longer feel obligated to do so by the reality of working for me.

Thanks to Beth and Joe Slevcove for allowing me the use of their peaceful home for the writing of this book. May you be blessed in knowing that your gift will impact the lives of parents and young teens across North America.

Thanks to Christina Robertson and Riptide, the middle school ministry of Journey Community Church, for continuing to let this geezer youth worker have real interaction with real middle schoolers. I'm honored to be a part of your wonderful ministry.

Thanks to Jeannie, Liesl, and Max, the most awesomest family ever. You are, and always will be, the best gift I have ever received.

And, thanks, God, for giving me this calling to middle schoolers. Seriously, I love it. You made me this way, and I am grateful.

Introduction

Thirteen-year-old Tracy was a straight-A student and a happy kid. She had loyal friends and a good relationship with her divorced mother, and seemed to be the embodiment of childhood innocence and happiness.

But all that changed, seemingly overnight. Tracy traded in her friends for new ones, and quickly moved into a life of sex, crime, violence (against others and herself), failing grades, and an off-the-charts belligerent attitude. Tracy's mother, Melanie, was beside herself. She tried everything she could think of, from grounding to conversation, from yelling to begging. Nothing worked. How could this sweet girl shift so instantly into a young woman apparently bent on destroying her life?

That was the plot of the 2003 award-winning film *Thirteen*. Directed by Catherine Hardwicke, and co-written by Hardwicke and teenager Nikki Reed (who also co-starred in the film), *Thirteen* shocked audiences and won praise for its apparent honesty and unflinching "this is how bad it can be" look into the life of a modern-day teen. While the movie dismantled the myth that young teens are still children, it strongly reinforced an emerging myth: that young teens will, overnight in most cases, switch from sweet and innocent children to brooding, terrifying parental nightmares.

Maybe this is why Mark Twain famously said, "When a child turns 12 you should put him in a barrel, nail the lid down and feed him through a knot hole. When he turns 16, plug the hole!" Twain also wrote, "When I was a boy of 14, my father was so ignorant I could hardly stand to have the old man around. But when I got to be 21, I was astonished at how much he had learned in seven years."

All this hoopla, all these myths, are constructed on an observable reality: Around the time of puberty, young teens begin a collection of radical changes, in body, mind, and soul. These changes can be horribly messy—and are the source of deep angst and upheaval for parents and teens alike.

And this is why parents of young teens need a deeper understanding.

The middle school years (11 to 14 years old) are one of the most misunderstood and underappreciated developmental periods of human life. Young teens are misunderstood by adults in general, to be sure; and they're misunderstood by churches more often than not. In my experience most conflict between parents and middle schoolers can be traced, after pulling back the onion-layers of behavior and tension, to a lack of understanding.

In most homes (whether Christian or not), middle schoolers are viewed either as children or as suddenly ready-for-the-world mini-adults. Of course, neither is fully true. We need a new and deeper understanding of the uniqueness of these transitionary years.

Culturally, there's been a *massive* shift in the last 20 years. As the age of puberty drops and youth culture becomes the dominant culture in our world, young teenagers are no longer living the waning years of an innocent childhood.[1] Decisions that used to be the stuff of high school—decisions that have enormous implications for the rest of life—are now played out daily in the lives of 12- and 13-year-olds. This has dramatically changed the nature of parenting young teens.

Not long ago most youth workers would have agreed that the high school years were the make-or-break space for the critical formation of youth. My contention (and I realize I'm biased by my calling and love for middle schoolers) is that this is no longer the case. These days, as a church youth worker, I often see high school ministry as being "corrective" in nature, while middle school ministry is now the make-or-break space (or "preventive" in nature). In the world of parenting teenagers, the middle school years set the direction, and parenting a high schooler—more often than not—is about (or, should be about) staying the course and moving teenagers toward independence.

There's a complicated and messy intersection of realities playing out in the world of young teens. It's the penultimate period of change in the lifespan of a human being,[2] combined with two other factors:

A culture that obsesses about everything "youth"—teenagers (including young teens) are marketed to more than ever and have a greater influence on adults than ever before (an influence we've granted them).

A culture flooded with information—anything and everything is readily available at the click of a mouse (and often thrust upon youth even without mouse-clicking).

It's unprecedented, really, how—in a shockingly short span of years—the middle school years have become such an epicenter for activity with lifelong implications. Normally this kind of human developmental change takes place over centuries.

A Bit of My Own Story

I'm writing this book from my life and experience, as well as my research. I write from my passion, and I hope this book has a conversational tone to it. I'm not an academic, and this isn't intended to be a true academic book—though I certainly hope it'll be helpful in academic settings. I'm a practitioner of middle school ministry—a guy who feels a calling to this age group, and has worked with them for almost 30 years.

Really, I'm just a guy who loves middle schoolers. They energize me. I find young teens to be life giving. I believe they're fun and insightful and capable of so much more reflection and world-shaping than most people give them credit for. Every word in this book pours out of that perspective, that affection.

So I thought it might be helpful for you to know just a tiny bit of my own story...

I grew up in youth group, in a large church in the Detroit area. My own experience in middle school (and high school) plays a huge role in my shaping and calling. I was a fairly lonely kid at school, but church (and, specifically, my church's youth ministry) was a safe place of belonging for me. The youth ministry at my church also gave me ample opportunities to develop leadership, to try things and fail, and to experience grace.

By the time I was a senior in high school, I had a sense that I should become a youth pastor, and I went to college pursuing that call. My youth internship and volunteer work were mostly with middle school kids (perhaps by default, since I was so close in age to the high schoolers). And when my new wife, Jeannie, and I started volunteering in the youth ministry where I'd eventually get my first paid role in ministry, the church had more need in the middle school area than in high school, so we ended up there.

I began working part time as a "junior high pastor," and I quickly fell in love with it. As I worked with this age group more, I began to discover through both study and experience many of the realities expounded on in this book. Plus, my personality just seemed more akin to young teens than older teens. All that began to draw me into a sense of lifelong calling to young teen ministry.

I worked in a few more churches as a full-time junior high pastor. And along the way, my thinking about middle schoolers and middle school ministry was stretched and challenged and deepened. I made lots of stupid mistakes, learned how easy middle schoolers are to manipulate, and saw countless misconceptions played out and then smashed.

A dozen years ago, I started working with Youth Specialties, a ministry that trains, resources, and encourages youth workers. But I could not, and would not, move away from my calling to middle schoolers, and I've been a volunteer middle school youth worker ever since. (These days I lead an eighth-grade boys' small group that meets weekly.) My time at Youth Specialties (which ended in late

2009), and my current consulting work with churches and coaching with youth workers, has given me a broad glimpse into the lives of tens of thousands of middle schoolers, as I've connected with thousands of others who share my calling.

What began as a generalized calling to youth ministry, roughly 30 years ago, is now a calling I hope and pray will play out in my life for many more years.

Oh, and I have two teenagers living in my own home: As I write this, my daughter, Liesl, is 17 and entering twelfth grade; my son, Max, is 13 and entering eighth grade. So the realities of my three decades of work with young teens get stretched, challenged, and confirmed every day.

What This Book Won't Cover

There are some wonderfully helpful parenting books out there. Most of them offer an *approach* to parenting, as well as practical implications and suggestions. This book is different. I'm not going to suggest an approach (unless you consider trying to understand better what's going on with your middle schooler to be an "approach"). I'm not going to give you suggestions for family prayer times or vacations, or tell you how to get your son to clean his room. It's not that I don't have those ideas and suggestions. But there are other books for that, and I don't want this book to run on to four hundred pages (nor do you!).

This book is unique in its purpose and scope, I think. My working assumption, my foundational theory, is this: If you understand why your young teen thinks, acts, and feels the way he or she does, you'll be in a significantly better place from which to engage with your child. And that's the bottom line during the teen years— staying engaged and keeping lines of communication open. Developing a better understanding of your young teen will impact everything you do as a parent, from boundary setting to consequence enforcement, from conversation attempts to homework help, and even from family prayer times to vacations.

A Few Words about Terminology

I've chosen to use the terms *young teen* and *middle schooler* as the primary ways of referring to the age group we'll focus on throughout this book. As I peruse the American scene, *middle school* seems to represent the dominant terminology and framing. But don't get hung up by that terminology if your church or schools still use *junior high* or some other term. Canada seems to almost exclusively use "junior high"; and in the United Kingdom, neither of these terms makes much sense, and young teens are usually just referred to as "11 to 14s." I'll also use *early adolescence* (or *early adolescents*), and, occasionally, *teens* (which I've found middle schoolers like to be called, but high schoolers hate).

Much of the media has started using the word *tween* (short for "in-between," and a cute version of "teen"), but I believe this term is often more confusing.[3] This word was originally used to describe the group I'd call "preteens" (10- and 11-year-olds, or fifth and sixth graders). But now it's often used (wrongly, I believe) in place of *young teen*. Since there's overlap between a preteen concept of fifth and sixth graders and a middle school notion of sixth through eighth graders, the terms and concepts get even more confusing. I'll mostly steer clear of the word *tweens* and use *preteens* when I'm writing about the kids just prior to puberty.

A Few Words about "A Few Words to Parents" Essays

After three decades in middle school ministry, I've developed a wonderful collection of dear friends who share my calling (though most of them are younger than me!). If there were some way all of us could sit in your living room and have a long chat, I'm sure it would be wonderful. Many of my friends have as much to say about middle schoolers as I do, and I wanted you to hear from some of them. So I've asked a handful of them to write short sidebars, with the almost-impossible task of choosing just one thing they'd like to say to parents of middle schoolers.

You'll find these essays scattered throughout the book under the title "A Few Words to Parents." They were written in response to one of two questions: "What's the one thing you wish parents understood about middle schoolers?" or, "What's one way you'd like to encourage parents of middle schoolers?"

My Prayers and Hopes for You

A couple of years ago, I co-authored with another middle school ministry expert a book for church youth workers (un)creatively titled, *Middle School Ministry.* Somewhere in the midst of writing that book, I knew I had to write a similar book for parents. As I speak to groups of parents about the subjects I'll address on the pages that follow, I often see their shoulders relax. They tell me how this new understanding has radical implications for their relationships with the middle schoolers in their homes.

My prayer is that this book will help you be energized in the challenging, sometimes wonderful, sometimes frightfully difficult God-given role you carry. I pray that as you read these pages, you will often be comforted, occasionally be stretched, and regularly gain new insight. And I pray the result will be improved communication with your young teen. Ultimately, my prayer is not primarily for you: My prayer is that this book will result in middle schoolers who love Jesus, because they're in a supportive and encouraging relationship with parents who model a love for Jesus. Mmm, may it be so.

When it comes to parenting middle schoolers, I don't have it all figured out (just ask my own kids!). But I'm a fellow traveler with you. And I've picked up a few things along the way that I hope you'll find helpful.

I hope you'll be inspired by what you read on these pages.

I hope your understanding of middle schoolers will dramatically increase and that this will lead to a strengthening of your parenting and a strengthening of the love in your home.

I hope your thinking will be pushed and prodded, that you'll see young teens in a new light and rethink some of your assumptions and parenting approaches.

I hope you'll experience multiple "Aha!" moments, where what you're reading suddenly makes sense of previously confounding behaviors and other realities you've experienced with middle schoolers.

I hope you'll formulate your own ideas about the practical stuff of parenting a young teen, new ways of approaching conversations and discipline and dispensing freedoms.

I hope you'll develop a language that will be useful for talking about young teens with other parents, teachers, church leaders, and even your own child.

I hope you'll sense God's great affection for you, and God's enjoyment of your desire to effectively parent the middle schooler in your home, whom God so deeply loves.

And I hope you'll be deeply encouraged—that you'll have a renewed sense of confidence that the ministry (good parenting is a ministry!) you're engaged in really does matter and really is making a difference (even when it doesn't feel like it).

I'm honored to come alongside you in this journey.

Marko

(that's what all my friends—and the world of youth workers—call me)

Chapter 1

Can Anything Good Come of This Age?

Derek was, well, a challenging kid to have in our middle school group. He was a natural leader, charismatic, and good looking. And he was disruptive. Not disruptive in an "Oh, he just needs to take his medication" way, or even in a "He has all the squirrelly characteristics of a young teen boy, turned to 11 on the dial" way. Derek was intentionally disruptive. His timid mom couldn't control him, and she had no idea what to do with him.

Smart and scheming, Derek would regularly manipulate entire hordes of boys and girls in our group into behaviors that would create havoc and get everyone except Derek in trouble with their parents. If there were a group of kids hiding somewhere in a stairwell, Derek was usually the kid who got them there. If students were caught smoking or drinking, then Derek was likely the provider. If all the kids in a certain section of the room were sitting with their arms crossed and "I dare you to teach me something" expressions firmly fixed on their faces, then they were almost assuredly imitating Derek.

I met many times with both Derek and his mom. I chatted with each of them on the phone frequently. I took Derek out for sodas and meals and showed him grace and love. I tried to help his mom with her challenging role of setting boundaries for him.

While there were certainly many factors involved, the struggle, as it pertained to Derek's disruption in our group, came down to two particularly vivid facts: 1) He didn't want to be there; and 2) his mom used attendance at our group as a punishment. She revealed this to me once, with only the tiniest bit of embarrassment. When she grounded him, he simply ignored it. When she took away other privileges, he either overrode her or manipulated her into reversing her decision. The only thing she'd ever found that "worked" was telling Derek he had to come to our church middle school group. And since he was almost always in trouble for something, we saw Derek fairly regularly.

I asked Derek's mom about this approach—more specifically, I asked if she thought it was healthy for Derek's spiritual development to experience church as a punishment. Her response was revealing: "I don't know what else to do. I can't handle him; when I send him to you, at least I don't have to worry about him for a few hours. I don't understand Derek at all, and I have no idea how to get through to him."

Natalie was another student in that same group. She was the youth group flirt. Her family was extremely active in our church, and she was present at everything we did. She wasn't overtly disruptive like Derek, but she was still exceedingly disinterested in anything other than constant chatting with friends, flirting with boys, and working on her next conquest.

In many ways, Natalie wasn't particularly unique—we had other girls (and guys) with the same values and behaviors. What made Natalie's situation stand out was her parents' perspective. One day they sat with me in my office, very frustrated, and asked, "Why can't you do something about Natalie? Why can't you change her? What's the point of our constantly bringing her to youth group if you can't fix her?" (To be fair, I'm not sure they actually used the word *fix*; but it was implied, even if they didn't use it.) But the most telling bit of the conversation was one sentence uttered by Natalie's mom: "She and her friends are nothing like I was at that age, and I don't understand her."

Yup, that's it in a nutshell. I've met with hundreds of parents during my years of middle school ministry, observed hundreds (or thousands) more, and often interact with parents of middle schoolers when I'm doing parenting seminars at churches. And this theme—this "I just don't understand my child" theme—is certainly common, if not nearly universal.

In fact, in my experience, just about the only parents of middle schoolers who think they *do* understand their child are those with an arrogant "What's there to understand?" attitude of indifference.

Common media portrayals of parents and young teens don't help. Parents are usually portrayed as bumbling and immature, while young teens (and teenagers in general) are often portrayed as savvier and smarter than their parents. I don't know about you, but I get really tired of the "doofus dad" stereotype I see on so much of the programming aimed at teenagers (as well as the "neurotic mom" stereotype).

But here's my observation: The gap between the perception many adults have of middle schoolers' potential and their actual potential is fairly wide. Most of this gap is rooted in complex cultural misunderstandings—even fear—of young teens.

I can't tell you how many times, over the years, I've been told by well-meaning church members and leaders: "God bless you for working with those kids; I sure couldn't do it." Or, "You must really be called to work with those kids because I can't understand how you do it."

I want to start this book by reframing a few things. And let's start with this one: The fact that you don't always understand your middle schooler is *not* cause for throwing in the towel, throwing your hands in the air, or any other defeatist metaphor involving throwing. The fact that you don't always understand your middle schooler is an *opportunity*. It's an opportunity to learn and grow; it's an opportunity to be dependant on God; it's an opportunity to get to know your son or daughter, all over again, during a time when your child really, really, really needs you to be present (even though he or she might be sending you signals to the contrary).

A Little History (Very Little, Actually)

Focused conversation and books (and ministry, for that matter) devoted to young teens is a fairly new phenomenon in our culture. And there's good reason for this. Until about the last 50 years or so, young teens weren't really considered "teens" at all.

Let's back way up. For thousands of years, in pretty much every culture around the world, children were children, and adults were adults. The line between these two worlds was clearly marked, and individuals were either on one side or on the other. Children participated in family and culture at large in culturally accepted, boundaried ways, and were encouraged to look toward, aspire to, and prepare for the day they'd cross the line into the adult community (which was usually around age 13 or 14 for girls, and 15 or 16 for boys).

Historically, every culture had some sort of rite of passage to mark the transition from childhood to adulthood.[1] Rites of passage are fairly nonexistent today. As a youth worker, when I ask teens how they'll know when they become adults, I get a wide range of responses, usually connected to some milestone: "When I get my driver's license" or "When I have sex for the first time" or "When I graduate from high school." When I ask parents, the responses are just as mixed and usually fall along the lines of "When they're responsible for themselves."

This response from parents makes sense, really. Since the stage of adolescence was first identified in the early twentieth century, "being responsible for oneself" has been the working definition of the end of adolescence (and the beginning of adulthood).[2] Adolescence was originally thought of as an 18-month window of time from age 14½; to 16—a bit of a culturally endorsed holding pattern in which "youth" were allowed an opportunity to wrestle with "adolescent issues." At the time, these issues were called "storm and stress" and were a simplified version of the independence issues we might characterize today. Over the years, while using various terminologies, they've sifted down to these three adolescent tasks: Identity ("Who am I?"), Autonomy ("How am I unique, and what power do I have?"), and Affinity ("Where and to whom do I belong?").[3] The shift that's taken place over the last hundred-plus years isn't really in the *definition* of adolescence, however. It's a shift in the *duration* of adolescence. And this has a direct impact, on many levels, on the existence and importance of middle school parenting.

By the time the 1970s rolled around, at least in the United States, adolescence was considered to be about five years long (or six school years)—extending from the commonly understood starting age of 13 to the normal graduation-from-high-school age of 18. Let's stop to think where these numbers came from, because they've been burned into our cultural consciousness for so many years.

Between the early twentieth century (when adolescence was first identified as an 18-month window) and the 1970s, the period of adolescence had expanded on both the opening and closing ends. The delaying of the end of adolescence was cultural, to be sure, and was directly tied to the normalization of high school education. In the earliest parts of the twentieth century, only a small percentage of older teenagers were in school. In fact, if older teens were in school at that point, most were already off to college; and this opportunity was primarily reserved for wealthier families.

High schools became more commonplace in the United States toward the end of the first half of the twentieth century, to the point that it was compulsory through 16 years old and culturally normative through 18 years old. By the time youth culture came into its own, in the 1950s, high schools were the norm. High schools, of course, became the boiler room of the new youth culture and quickly aided in raising the age at which adolescents were expected to be fully functioning contributors to society (the upper end of adolescence).

But the beginning age of adolescence also changed during this time period. At the turn of the twentieth century, when adolescence was first talked about, the average age for the onset of puberty was 14.5 years old.[4] This physical change became the de facto starting point for adolescence. But between 1900 and 1970, the average age for the onset of puberty dropped by about a year and a half, to 13 years old.

To say this change in age for the beginning of adolescence was purely physiological would be incomplete. As youth culture found anchoring and validation, younger kids (who were 12 and 13 at the time, sometimes even 14) aspired to be a part of what was ahead of them. Soon enough, these preteens were considered young teens, both physiologically and culturally.

Now, this may not be a surprise to you, but things have changed dramatically since 1970. I could write separate books about how the world has changed, how adolescence has changed, how education has changed, and how physiology has changed over the last four decades. I'll keep it short, but let's start with the older end of adolescence.

Since the 1970s, the expected age of integration into adult life has continued to grow older. There are economic reasons for this,[5] cultural reasons for this,[6] and physiological and psychological reasons for this[7] (and probably other contributing factors). It's hard to nail down an exact age, as high school graduation provided us. Yet those who study adolescence commonly understand it as extending well into the late twenties now, on average.

But this book isn't about older teenagers. So let's focus on the beginning of adolescence.

The average age of puberty has continued to drop. These days, girls begin developing breast buds and pubic hair as early as 9.5 or 10 years old, and they often experience menarche (their first period) around age 11 or 12. For our purposes, it's fair to say that puberty now begins around age 11.[8]

I'll talk more about why this has happened in chapter 3. But for now, let's deal with this reality: Adolescence begins around 11 years old. And that's just physiologically. Culturally, young teens have become fully ensconced in youth culture at younger ages also, creating a calcifying edge to this new, younger definition of a teenager.

In fact, the lengthening of adolescence to a 15-years-plus journey has caused many to start talking about the adolescent experience in three phases: Young teen, mid-teen, and older teen (or emerging adulthood).[9] Add to this the "youthification" of preteens (often called "tweens" by the media these days), and it would be fair to say the adolescent journey is closer to 20 years long—a full fourth of life. Now that should reshape our thinking about parenting teenagers in general, and parenting young teens specifically.

A Rare Opportunity

When I talk to middle school youth workers, I frame the rare opportunity of middle school ministry in terms of the overlap of these two variables:

1. Research shows that most believers (the *vast* majority) begin their journey of faith *prior to* the age of 13 or 14.[10] This is certainly reflective of the reality that most decisions of faith are made during childhood. But there seems to be enough "childhood" left in young teens that they are still very spiritually open, and the likelihood of conversion drops off dramatically after the young teen years.

2. The two years following the onset of puberty (remember: Average age = 11) are a tumultuous period of change. One of the most dramatic of these changes is the onset of abstract thinking, which is essential to owning one's faith.

In other words—I tell youth workers—the young teen years are an unprecedented opportunity by the very nature of the overlap of childhood and young adulthood. Childlike openness, combined with (semi-)adult-like thinking ability; willingness combined with exploration.

But I'd like to shift that language a bit for you, as a parent. I think there's an even more significant overlap occurring during the young teen years, when it comes to parenting:

1. You are still the number one influence in the life of your son or daughter. Did you catch that? Read it again.

2. The two years following the onset of puberty (remember: Average age = 11) are a tumultuous period of change. One of the most dramatic of these changes is the onset of abstract thinking, which is essential to owning one's identity.

Let's unpack that a bit. First, that statement about your being the number one influence in the life of your son or daughter. It sure might not feel like that's true. All the real-life evidence in your home might cause you to think you've lost that influence. But don't be misled by the behavior of your teen. For years, I taught both youth workers and parents that, during the young teen years, the peer group begins to eclipse parents' influence. But that's just not the case—and research has born this out time and time again.[11]

There is no question that the peer group begins to play a more significant role in the life of your young teen; but you're still in the top spot, influence-wise. It's not until the later years of high school that peer influence starts to eclipse parent influence, with peer influence clearly taking the lead during emerging adulthood.

My two-word implication: *Have hope.* Okay, four more words: *Don't squander your influence.*

Now you likely noticed that the second of those two overlapping factors is the same in the parent mix as in the youth worker mix. But it's not quite the same. I changed out the last word, from "owning one's faith" to "owning one's identity." Here's why: The primary role of church youth workers is the faith formation of teens. But your parenting role, and your opportunity, is to influence the much broader and all-encompassing reality of identity (which includes faith, but is more than that).

How Should You Respond?

You might feel I overuse this term in this book, but I'll sum up my parenting advice to you with one word: *Engagement.* Counter to the many external indicators you might be experiencing, these are *not* the years for you to disengage or pull back. Just the opposite: These are years for you to lean in. In many ways, these years are your last shot. By the time your son or daughter is 16 or so, much of who he or she is—and will be in the future—is set in wet cement.

Think of parenting a young teen as your final, big, uphill push in the road-race of your God-given role. Not that it's all a downhill coast after the young teen years. But your influence will decline, your child will have more independence (and "own" more of his or her choices), and the bulk of your work will be finished.

But the final, big, uphill push on a road-race is the most difficult. You'll be weary at times. You'll be confused. You'll have your buttons pushed and your own weaknesses exposed. Add to this "encouraging" portrait the reality that there are no guarantees. I've seen disengaged parents whose children have stellar character and a passion for God; and I've seen wonderful engaged parents whose children choose horrible paths in life, leading to pain and misery. But, on average, the older teenagers I see who are comfortable with who they are, confident in their beliefs, and ready to step into adulthood, are those whose parents, with humility and dependence on God, attempted to stay engaged and walk alongside their children.

My middle school son and I take Kung Fu lessons together. Our instructor is always harping on the need to have "martial spirit." When we feel like giving up, or slowing down, he reminds us of this, usually unpacking it while emphasizing the results we'll get if we push through, step it up, and work through the pain. I think you can see the connection here.

Okay. Let's move forward. Parenting a middle schooler is a beautiful gauntlet of complexity, and an amazing opportunity. Let's do this thing.

A FEW WORDS TO PARENTS

YOU'RE NOT ALONE!

Do you remember how alone you felt as a middle school student, when all those changes were going on in your body, mind, and soul? I remember wondering if I was the only one experiencing these weird sensations in my body, and these weird situations in life. I remember wondering if I was normal, if I was going to survive, and if I was ever going to come out of the mess I was living through.

Interestingly enough, I'm having those same feelings 30 years later as a parent of middle schoolers. Sometimes my kids drive me crazy. Sometimes I lose my patience (okay, more than sometimes on that one). Sometimes I wonder whether my kids are just going through a phase, or are they developing lifelong character flaws? Sometimes I question if I am doing a good job as a parent, or if I'll survive the teenage years of my kids.

Some of these troubling feelings and thoughts are way too similar to the struggles I had when I was 13. But what I have come to find, as I've talked to other parents of middle school students, is the same truth I discovered as an awkward 13-year-old: I am not alone! And neither are you!

You are not alone! Every parent of middle schoolers is feeling the same way you are. All (decent) parents of young teens question their ability to parent, their approach, their reactions, their discipline system, and their kids' responses. Everyone! You are not alone! None of us have this parenting thing figured out (and those who say they do are either lying or delusional). The journey of parenting is difficult, and it doesn't even get much easier with experience, because even if you think you've got it figured out with kid number one, you find kid number two is different. You have to start all over again.

What do you do? Be open and honest with someone. I've found in recent years that when you get parents of middle schoolers together in a room, if one parent is willing to say, "Hey, my kid seems to lie all the time—does anyone else deal with this?" the rest of the parents in the room quickly chime in with, "Oh, yeah, I thought we were the only ones who struggled with that! What are you doing to help your child with this?" When you get parents talking with one another about parenting middle schoolers, great encouragement flows freely, and most people leave the conversation recharged to continue the joys (and frustrations) of raising a teenager to be a godly young man or woman.

As a fellow parent, I want to strongly encourage you to seek places where you can be honest about the challenges you face in parenting, and find others who are willing to do the same. Ask your youth pastor if he or she will facilitate some forums on parenting where parents can talk and share with one another. And be encouraged—you are NOT alone; you may just be the only one willing to admit you're not perfect.

—Alan Mercer is the pastor of middle school ministries
at Christ Community Church in Leawood, Kansas.

Chapter 2

It's All about Change

I'm always a little bit surprised by how many parents of middle schoolers have never read anything about the development of young teens. (Give yourself a pat on the back for being an exception, even if this is your first book of this type.) Most parents assume they already "get it," since they were once young teens themselves. They assume nothing has really changed (other than, like, the Internet, and other insignificant stuff like that), and quickly adopt the attitude toward young teens projected by media ("they're strange, ungrateful, and don't need you anymore"), or the attitude projected by many schools and our government ("they're helpless little children who need to be protected and sheltered"). We parents all learn—even if it's not our normal predisposition—to wing it. We learn to adjust on the fly, to accept odd behaviors, strange smells, and awkward clothing choices. We get passive in our parenting, or we get desperate. Neither is helpful. Both lead to disengagement.

Anyhow, it's really, really common for parents of young teens not to know much about early adolescent development. Yet I'm convinced that understanding middle schoolers is the second most important thing you can do to increase your effectiveness as a parent.

Yeah, it's the second most important thing. So we'll return to it in a couple of paragraphs.

The *most* important thing you can do to increase your effectiveness, as a Christian parent of a middle schooler, is to deepen your own connection to God. See, parenting a middle schooler flows out of who you are, not what you know. You can have all the best tricks for getting conversation going, an almost mystical ability to motivate your child, a deep understanding of middle schoolers, and the relational ability of Oprah Winfrey, but if you aren't authentically and deeply connected to God, how would you stand a chance of pointing kids in God's direction?

But this chapter is really about the second most important thing you can do to increase your effectiveness in parenting a young teen. And that, as I've said, is to understand young teens. Deeply.

I've been working with and studying young teens for about three decades. And I can honestly say that while I've learned a ton about kids in that time, I still feel as though I'm always learning new stuff.

Early adolescence is a profoundly unique period of human development. Really, it's just astounding how much is going on and how different it is from other developmental life stages.

Where most people go wrong (especially those who don't work with young teens or don't care about them) is in making one of two assumptions. And historically, most cultures have erred in one of these two directions.

The first extreme is to assume young teens are just little adults. (Or, that they are little versions of high schoolers, which is slightly different, but still inaccurate.) Young teens seem like teenagers in many ways, and they certainly want to be treated like teenagers and don't want to be perceived as children. So we parents capitulate to culture—and to the premature desire of kids themselves—and assume they're slightly smaller versions of ourselves (or slightly smaller versions of their older siblings).

Historically, the United States, Canada, and the United Kingdom have treated young teens this way (at least for the last couple of hundred years). And with a media culture that serves up more of what young teen consumers want, this perception has deepened in recent decades.

The other extreme, of course, is the assumption that young teens are really just oversized children. This, for many reasons, seems to be the default in lots of churches. I believe this often comes from a desire to protect young teens from rushing into adulthood and adult-like behaviors. In some ways this is a good motivation, and it carries some developmentally appropriate freight. But it can also be misguided—an overprotection that stunts the growth of kids during this critical transitionary time of life.

The dealio, as I've clearly tipped my hand, is that neither of these extremes is especially helpful.

One-Word Definition

If I asked you to summarize the young teen experience in only one word, what would you choose? I've asked this question from time to time during seminars and conversations, and here are a few common responses I've heard:

Stressed	Emerging
Immature	Spontaneous
Confused	Unpredictable
Impossible	Challenging-but-full-of-possibility (People always try to get away with strings of hyphenated words when you ask for just one.)
Annoying	
Fun	
Potential	
Eager	

If you asked me (Go ahead and ask. Say it out loud: "Marko, if you were to describe the young teen experience in one word, what word would you choose?"), I'd respond calmly: "Change."

Change.

That's it, in a word. The life of a middle schooler is *all about* change. As previously noted, it's the second most significant period of change in the human lifespan. Stepping into puberty, and the two or three years that follow, brings about cataclysmic change in pretty much every area of life. It's a deeply radical seismic shift that upends everything that was and ushers in a period of profound instability.

Think of a significant change you've experienced in your adult life—maybe a move or a new job. Remember how you felt during that time? You probably experienced a combination of uneasiness (from fear of the unknown) and excitement (from the prospect of what could be). That's very much akin to the experience of early adolescence.

But the difference between a significant change you may have experienced as an adult and the significant change young teens are slogging through is this: Your feelings associated with change are mostly due to external factors. You likely experienced all kinds of internal stuff as a result of the external factors. But for young teens, the momentum of change is largely internal (although most young teens experience a host of external changes—such as a new school, new youth group, new friends, new freedoms—that further radicalize the internal stuff). The massive tsunami of change in the life of a 13-year-old is developmental, stemming from physical, cognitive, emotional, relational, and spiritual changes that are taking place in their bodies and minds.

Back in the '70s, a psychologist named Stephen Glenn came up with a helpful little description of this change that I've found useful and have modified here:[1]

Birth to 2 years old = **Sampling**

3 to 7 years old = **Testing**

8 to 10 years old = **Concluding**

* **Puberty** *

11 to 14 years old = **Sampling**

15 to 19 years old = **Testing**

20+ years old = **Concluding**[2]

Let's unpack that a bit. Glenn suggested there's a parallel between the childhood years and the teenage years when it comes to acquiring, processing, testing, and making conclusions about the world. Babies are intake experts. They're constantly sampling the world around them by watching, listening, touching, and, of course, inserting everything that can possibly fit—as well as some things that won't—into their mouths. For them, the world is a sampler platter.

Then there are those wild middle-childhood years. (By the way, the age brackets on this model are not hard and fast—they're fuzzy and vary from kid to kid.) If you have younger children, or if you think back to an earlier period of your young teen's life, you can see how children shift into a phase of testing. It's not quite as simple as their taking the information they've been gathering for two years and sending it all off to the Research and Development department in their brains. But it's close.

You can see this testing work in the following behaviors:

- Pushing you on boundaries and rules
- Testing different approaches to getting things ("Now I'm demanding what I want" and "Now I'm the sweet kid, charming you into compliance")
- Making gregarious, exclamatory comments to see how you respond
- Jumping around on things, knocking things together, pulling things apart

But in late childhood, there's a dramatic shift. The pre-adolescent, pre-abstract mind begins to be amazingly self-impressed. The pre-teen brain is like a high-end horse-and-buggy in the early 1900s. The early twentieth century was the absolute peak for the horse and buggy, in terms of technology—but the age of the automobile was just around the corner.[3] That's what's going on in the minds of young teens: They have the concrete thinking thing down—but this wonderfully refined mindset is on the verge of being outdated.

In the final pre-adolescent stage, children wrap up their testing phase and move full-bore into concluding. For example, ask a 10-year-old to give you input on a complex societal issue—such as racism or poverty or foreign trade—and, if she understands the question, she'll have a solution. What you will *not* hear is, "Well, that's complex, and I'm not sure I have a solution." What you *will* hear is something that starts with, "They should just…." Of course, it likely won't be a workable solution, although 10-year-olds can be surprisingly insightful (since they don't get bogged down in the hip-deep mud of complexities).

The same goes for spiritual stuff. Preteens are famous for drawing conclusions about all things spiritual. They really should be employed as marketers because they're fantastic at making overly simplistic, conclusive decrees. Their spiritual conclusions (which are age-appropriate, so this is not about immaturity) sound like bumper stickers.

But then (insert theme music from *Jaws*) along comes puberty, sneaking up on these confident and world-wise (in their minds, anyway) young teens. And all that beautiful conclusiveness gets annihilated.

In an era before we used the word *tsunami* as a metaphor for everything that changes, middle school ministry pioneer Wayne Rice described this onslaught as a tidal wave, wiping out all that hard work of sampling, testing, and concluding, and forever changing the landscape.

And then the three-step process starts all over again.

The young teen years—parallel to the earliest years of life— become, once again, a time of data collecting. Sampling. (It's interesting that these two stages of life, as mentioned earlier, are the two most dramatic times of change in a lifespan.)

The world is all-new to a young teen, thanks in part to new ways of thinking, new freedoms, increased access to information— including increased access to the world of adults—and an expanding worldview. Middle schoolers' new-again phase of sampling and information gathering is directly tied to the massive change that's going on in their lives.

Again, think of a significant change you've experienced as an adult (a move, a job change, a significant new relationship). Let's say you start a new job. Those early days of change are spent in information-gathering mode. *What are the workplace norms? How do I get from here to there? Who really has the power? Where are the paper clips stored? How do I fill out these forms for Human Resources?*

Even though much of this sampling and information gathering for middle schoolers takes place internally, we can also see tons of it working out in external ways:

- What kinds of clothes should I wear so I don't look like a little kid?
- How am I supposed to interact with my parents and friends?
- What sports and other hobbies might I be interested in doing or good at doing?
- Which subgroup of youth culture might be the right fit for me?

One night a couple of years ago, when the guys in my current middle school small group were just starting seventh grade, we were talking about what it means to be a man. We compared stereotypes of manliness with a look at true manhood. (Really, we were talking about wearing masks.) While filling out a silly "manliness quiz," we started talking about a sex question. Well, actually, it was a question about bragging about sexual experience.

I had four guys in my group—and they were split right down the middle, revealing a perfect snapshot of this age group. Two of the guys were extremely nervous to even talk about this subject. They stopped making eye contact, didn't joke around at all, and gave answers that would be parent-approved.

But the other two guys were nuts! Seriously. They went off, saying things like, "When am I *not* having sex?" and doing little hip thrusts and giggling maniacally.

Since I was in the process of writing about this topic, it dawned on me—right in the middle of that discussion—that I was witnessing two of those stages. Two of the boys were very much in the "concluding" mindset of upper elementary. And the other two boys were clearly experimenting with information gathering. They were "sampling" the responses of the other guys in the group and sampling the responses of my co-leader and me. They were sampling what it felt like to be a guy who talks about sex in over-the-top ways. (Neither of these guys actually had any sexual experience, by the way; they were just playing a role—a role created to gather information.)

Don't misunderstand this example: I'm not suggesting that concluding is about giving acceptable responses or that sampling is about bragging about sexual proclivities. That's not the point.

This sampling phase can be wonderful, full of opportunity and possibility. But it can also be (and almost always is, for most kids, at one point or another) scary and overwhelming. That's why this next section is so important.

Normalizing Your Young Teen's Experience

I'm convinced that one of the most important ministries you can have with your young teen is to normalize his or her experience. Here's what I mean: *Every* young teen, at one time or another, feels abnormal. They feel as though they're physically developing in the wrong way. Or they feel as though they're the only ones experiencing emotional swings. Or they feel as though their spiritual doubts are aberrant and unique.

Don't trivialize your child's experience. (For example, don't say something like, "Don't you realize that you're *not* unique? *All* kids your age are going through what you're going through.") Instead, help your young teen realize that his or her experience of change is normal—even good.

I will always remember an opportunity to normalize the emotional experience of my then 13-year-old daughter, Liesl. Here's how it happened.

Liesl and I were sitting at the kitchen table and having dinner together. (I'm not sure where my wife and son were.) In casual conversation, I asked about her homework.

She freaked. She exploded with, "Why are you yelling at me?"

A bit taken aback, I calmly responded, "Liesl, I'm not yelling. I'm just asking you about your homework."

Liesl escalated even more to a shrieking frenzy: "Stop yelling at me! I don't know why you're yelling at me!"

Now she was pushing my buttons, and I felt my own emotions starting to rise. I wasn't sure whether I should step into the role she was projecting on me and actually start yelling ("I'll show you yelling, if that's what you want!") or start laughing at her. I also knew, in a rare moment of parental insight, that neither of those responses would be helpful. But I could tell we weren't going to get anywhere at the moment, and we both needed a little space to cool down.

So I said, "I need you to go to your room. When you've calmed down, we can talk about this."

Liesl jumped up from the table, stomped across the house and up the stairs to her room, and slammed the door, yelling the entire time: "You're always yelling at me! It's so unfair!"

I waited, picking at my food.

Not three minutes passed before I heard her door open. Then I heard Liesl coming down the stairs, crying. "Daddy," she said, "I'm sorry." (*sniff, sniff*) "I don't know why I was yelling at you."

I saw a window of opportunity to normalize Liesl's experience. I asked her, "Would it be okay if I tried to explain what just happened?"

"Okay," she said through self-flagellating sniffs.

The rest of the conversation went something like this:

"Liesl, do you ever feel like your emotions are out of your control?"

"Yeah."

"Do you sometimes feel like you're depressed, and you don't know why?"

"Yeah." (*sniff*)

"And do you sometimes get totally excited but don't know where that came from either?"

"Totally! Emily and I get in trouble all the time at school because we get so excited we can't stop talking!"

I went on to explain to Liesl that when she was a kid, she had emotions, too. But her brain was a kid's brain, and she was only able to experience certain emotions. "It's like," I said, "you had a small set of emotional options, and you knew them well. But now that you're a teenager, your brain is changing." I explained that this meant she was able to experience many emotions that she couldn't before. But these emotions are new to her, and she's not used to them. I told her it was like getting a pair of new jeans that aren't broken in—they're still a little uncomfortable, and they feel like they don't belong to you yet.

I continued, "But here's the cool thing. Jesus promises us, in John 10:10, that he came to give us 'a full life.' In order for you to really experience a full life, you need a whole range of emotions. This change you're going through with your emotions is a change God invented. It's a little awkward while you're going through it; but it's all part of God's love for you."

Liesl and I talked about it for a bit more, and then we moved on to something else (maybe her homework?).

We must always be ready to slip "It's okay," "It's normal," and "It's good" into our conversations with our young teens. These statements constantly remind them that their changes are normal and good and that they'll turn out great. And they really do need to be reminded of this over and over and over again. (Of course, they'll only hear it when they are ready to hear it, which is why we need to say it with regularity.)

In the coming chapters, I'll unpack in more detail how these different changes play out in the lives of young teens.

A FEW WORDS TO PARENTS

YOUR KID IS NORMAL

I figured out a way to get filthy rich in youth ministry: Convince a group of investors to pay me $100 every time I utter the phrase "Your kid is normal" to concerned parents. In no time, I would not only have extra coin in my 401(k), but I would also be speaking four words of truth and life to those parents.

Your kid is normal. That's a phrase you can hold onto as your young teen navigates the world of early adolescence. Maybe you're the parent whose young teen just entered the wonderful world of puberty, and went from being your best friend to (what feels like) your biggest enemy. Or maybe you're the parent whose oldest kid just flew through his or her teenage years with little to no drama. You were ready to write your first of many books on parenting because you'd found the golden ticket to raising the perfect teenager; that is, until kid number two came around and blew up the perfect world created by kid number one! Or maybe you're the parent who can't figure out why your middle schooler is so respectful to everyone else in the world—except you!

I could go on and on painting situations and scenarios that normal parents with normal kids wade through. Nine times out of 10, when parents ask me, "What's wrong with my kid?" my answer is, "Nothing. Your kid is normal."

—Nate Severson is the middle school youth pastor at Hillcrest Covenant Church in Prairie Village, Kansas.

Chapter 3

Walking Hormones?
(Physical and Sexual Development)

The setting: A tiny, hot, boy-smell-drenched small group room at church.

The context: My middle school guys' small group—all sixth graders.

The conversation:

Me: "So Potiphar's wife…"

Shane: "Oh! I've heard this! Isn't she the one that said Joseph raped her?"

Me: "Yeah, that's right. She wanted Joseph to have sex with her…"

Matt: "We're starting sex ed next week in school."

Shane: "We did it in our class a few weeks ago."

Zack: "You *did it* in sex ed?"

(*Giggles all around.*)

Zack: "That must be a new teaching method!"

Shane: "Ha! No, I don't think our teachers have a license to do that."

Zack (*very serious, to me*): "You need a license to have sex?"

Me: "Yeah."

Zack: "Really?"

Me: "You have to apply for one down at the DMV."

Zack: "Really?"

Me: "No. Back to Potiphar's wife…"

The guys joked about needing a "sex license" for the next three years that we were in a small group together.

Hormones Are about More Than Sex

Lots of people characterize the teenage years as a time when we're taken over by hormones. You've probably even heard people refer to young teens as "walking bundles of hormones." There's some truth in this. And there's some inaccuracy also.

First, the truth: While I don't believe the physical changes are the most significant changes young teens are experiencing (especially in terms of the implications for parenting and faith development), the physical changes are still a *huge* deal. And, chronologically, they're the first of many interdependent aspects of change.

Physical change starts with hormones.

Actually, that's not completely accurate either. Puberty starts in the brain. At some moment in time, the early-adolescent brain says, "Now seems to be the time to open the hormonal floodgates." The brain signals the testes (for boys) or the ovaries (for girls) to start creating and releasing hormones.[1]

This is the launch point of the tsunami of change we've been talking about. And so begin the physiological changes (all the body and brain stuff) and the results of those physiological changes (cognitive, relational, emotional, worldview, and faith).

So, in a sense, yes—the change of early adolescence is about hormones.

But in another sense, it's really not about hormones—at least not in the way people popularly interpret that. When most people talk about hormones and the changes they bring, they're really only talking about one aspect of adolescence: Obsession with sex.

It's wrong (and unfair) to characterize young teens as being sex-obsessed, and it's really important to realize when we're doing it. Because when such a caricature infiltrates our thinking to the point where we believe it's the whole story, it diminishes the importance of other, nonsexual changes that are going on in middle schoolers' lives.

The Scope of Physical Change

Young teens are intrigued by—even proud of—the changes going on in their bodies, while also being nervous, sheepish, and confused about those physical changes.

Young teens *want* to grow up (at least most of them do). And they *want* to have the bodies of adults—or at least their idealized notions of what an adult body is like.

Sure, they're experiencing physical change in their girl parts and boy parts (or, as I've heard boy parts referred to, their "hanging down parts," their "junk," their "stuff," their "crotchal region," their "package," and many other inventive phrases not fit for printing here), but their physical changes are, of course, much more than that.

Hair in New Places

During the earliest phases of puberty, hair starts growing in places where young teens have never had hair before—the pubic area, armpits, face, and legs. This process usually continues throughout adolescence.

I remember this hair-growing thing quite vividly from my own young teen experience, due to a rather unfortunate assumption I made. In about seventh grade, I'd noticed a good amount of dark hair growing on the lower part of my legs, between my knees and ankles. I thought this was completely cool and totally manly, and I wanted to do anything in my power to assist the process.

This being the 1970s, I wore those tube socks that came up to my knees. And, since I didn't have any leg hair growing *above* my knees, my early adolescent mind concluded that leg hair must grow best "in the dark" (where my legs were shielded by my glorious socks). There must have been a bit of leftover memory from a botany experiment we'd done in elementary school, where we found that a plant kept in the dark of a classroom closet grew really fast but didn't last.

I grew up in Detroit, where the summers were notoriously hot and muggy. But I went through an entire Detroit summer wearing jeans—not shorts—because I was convinced I needed to keep my legs "in the dark." The funny thing was that my leg hairs—even above my knees—did grow in that summer. And I thought I *made it happen.* I was very proud of my accomplishment, and it took every bit of restraint I had not to prance around my school that fall in shorts, while pointing to my legs and saying, "Look what I did this summer!"

While this hair-growth thing might be something guys (more so than girls) are proud of when it comes to armpits and upper-lip peach fuzz, both girls and guys tend to have polarized responses to pubic hair. They want it—but they're a bit freaked out by it. Spending time with middle schoolers at a retreat or camp where they have to get dressed in a communal environment will reveal that they tend to have one of two extreme responses. Those who develop a little later will usually be shy (I've seen hundreds of guys get changed *inside* their sleeping bags). Kids who develop a little earlier than their peers may be equally shy—or they swing the pendulum (no pun intended) to the other extreme, walking around naked like proud lions and casually showing off their newfound glory to anyone and everyone.

Because the "hair thing" is such a visible change, it can also become an area of teasing (either for "too much" or "too little" hair). Quick point: Of all the things I'm going to encourage you to talk about with your young teen, tread lightly here. Moms shouldn't mention this with their sons, and dads definitely shouldn't with their daughters. Even if you're the same gender as your child, never mention this with anyone else around; and never-ever-*ever* tease, even if you mean it in a good natured way. If you do mention it, remember that "normalizing" concept, and talk about it in a very matter-of-fact voice, inviting questions.

Body Shape and Height

Of course, the physical changes are about much more than hair growth. The young teen's body shape changes (shoulders, chest, waist, muscle mass, and so much more), in addition to experiencing crazy spurts in height.

The whole area of vertical growth is another sticky one. Boys who grow taller are usually pleased with this, to a point. Some of the tallest boys may worry that they're too far outside the bell curve and quickly tire of being known only as "the tall guy." Shorter guys start to obsess over their height and can really suffer a bit of a young teen identity crisis over what it means to be the short guy.

It's so easy for even the most well-meaning parent to occasionally crack a sideways joke about a short son or daughter. Remember, this can be seriously damaging. We need to be passionate about affirmation and normalization—not allowing for even a peep of teasing. What seems like a harmless offhanded tease to you can easily compound a child's suspicion that something is wrong with him or her.

Guys tend to be more concerned about being too short because our culture tells them guys are supposed to be big, tough, and macho. Girls, on the other hand, tend to be more concerned with being too tall because our culture tells them they're supposed to be diminutive and petite (unless they're supermodels!). Much of this stems from the fact that girls, on average, hit puberty 18 months prior to boys. So girls start growing taller at an earlier age. Add to this the fact that girls usually reach their full adult height before high school graduation, while boys often continue growing taller well into their early twenties. Girls who will eventually be above-average height are almost universally taller than their male peers in sixth and seventh grade. This is rarely something they're pleased with, and they're often teased about it (at worst) or have it constantly pointed out (at best). Have we talked about normalization yet?

Breast and Penis Size

Let's get the easier of these two out of the way first: Guys obsess about the length (or lack of length) of their penises. Anyone who receives email spam about miraculous penis-lengthening solutions knows this doesn't seem to be limited to adolescent guys. But because a guy's body is changing so dramatically, he knows he's supposed to get an adult-sized penis—whatever that is. It's not uncommon (in fact, it's the norm, rather than the exception) for middle school guys to be very aware of the length of their penises, both in a flaccid and erect condition. Their trusty school ruler becomes a measuring stick of choice.

But there are three reasons that penis size is less of an issue for middle school guys than breast development is for middle school girls.

1. Guys are secretive about this, and when they aren't being secretive, they usually lie. They'll talk about penis length, but normally it's in third person or in the form of a lie.
2. Guys are less verbal than girls, which means lots of guys never talk about this kind of stuff with anyone, let alone a parent.
3. The length of a guy's penis is almost always hidden (which is part of why communal changing and showering, such as at a camp setting, can be such a big issue for guys), unlike a girl's breast development, which is pretty much out there for everyone to see, despite clothes to provide cover.

Girls know breast development is a big part of their changing bodies (clearly boys know that, too). And, boy howdy, does it ever cause drama, concern, fear, obsession, and plenty of visual inspection. Here's a condensed and oversimplified rule: Girls want to be in the middle of the normal distribution. Breasts that are "too large" or that develop "too early" can bring all kinds of unwanted attention and teasing. (This attention is occasionally desired, which often points to other issues about the girl's relationship with males in general.)

As with most physical changes in young teens, it's pretty difficult to find the girl who believes her breast development is normal. Our culture (and their own culture) really puts them in a catch-22 on this one. They've learned that having breasts of a normal or slightly-larger-than-normal size is culturally desirable. But girls with larger or earlier developing breasts are often made to feel abnormal, as if they should be ashamed. Peers (guys and girls both) will assume they're "loose"—as if that has something to do with breast development. And then there's the ever-present concern girls have that one of their breasts is larger than the other and that they'll always be "deformed" or lopsided.

The intensity and concern is only a fraction less intense for girls who develop breasts later than their peers. Being "flat chested" brings teasing from boys and girls alike and is a constant source of worry for these girls. Their concern (and, for some, full-on obsession) about their lack of breast development would be an issue for them *even if there were no teasing.* But the teasing thing—which is an almost universal experience for late-blooming girls—ratchets this issue up one-hundredfold.

Obviously, moms will have more opportunity to speak directly to this with their daughters, affirming their beauty, encouraging them that they'll catch up, and dismantling (to the best of your ability) our cultural obsession with body shape (in general) and breasts (in particular). Dads can play a role here also—we just have to be much more careful about what we do and don't say. (If you're a single dad, your primary role is to make sure your daughter has a woman she can talk with about this stuff.)

There are also some young teen girls who see puberty and their changing bodies as a nuisance; they'd rather just be "one of the guys." They can tell guys are looking at them differently and are starting to treat them differently. And this isn't a welcome change. They enjoyed the more level playing field of the preteen years, when they could be friends with boys without sexual identity playing a significant role in the relational mix. They don't want to be seen as objects, or they don't want to be one of those "girlie girls," obsessed with outward appearance. They want to be equals on the soccer field and in the classroom, as well as in friendships. Physical development— particularly for girls—can completely disrupt this equilibrium, and this change can be unwelcome.

This is a tough one because we parents can't change the reality that male-female relationships are shifting as kids enter their middle school years, and that some of this shift is due to physical changes. What we *can* do is affirm their desire to downplay the change. Support their attempts to have nonsexualized friendships. And be extra careful not to make little comments that imply they should be "more feminine," thereby playing into the cultural stereotypes and rushing their fragile developmental transition.

A disclaimer: After three decades of middle school ministry experience and one experience with a (very verbal and blunt) young teen girl in my own home, I can say I've never had even one conversation with a teenage girl about breasts. I shouldn't have such conversations—and I don't. (Got that, men?) But we men still play a key role, since girls are taking tons of cues from all the males in their lives—their dads in particular—about who they are and who they're becoming. Affirm your daughter like crazy—but go light on the physical stuff. Let her know you think she's beautiful; but more than that, affirm her character, personality, and questions—affirm anything and everything you can. Help her see that men find there's more to them than their physical exterior. This can have a huge and profound effect on her identity formation, including her sexual identity formation.

Moms: This is one of those areas where, when the time is right, you absolutely must normalize the experience of your daughter. You need to talk with her about this stuff. I'm not suggesting you need to schedule appointments with your daughter to have "breast talks." But you should take advantage of natural opportunities in conversation (like, while shopping for clothes). Of course, if you notice your daughter is struggling with this—either because she's flaunting or because she's getting teased—take the opportunity to bring up the subject in a discreet and appropriate context. (Again, single dads, be intentional about identifying a woman, or women, your daughter can talk with.)

Changing Voices

We tend to think of voice changing as a guy thing. But both girls and boys experience changes in the tone of their voices during the young teen years. If you listen to a fifth-grade girl talking with an eighth-grade girl, you'll hear it. The shift is just more pronounced in boys.

And a shifting voice doesn't seem to be an area of concern for girls. (Thank God for one area of physical change that doesn't cause them distress.) But for guys, this one is right up there with height—it's a big one!

Observationally, I'd say this change in guys is one where the bell curve (or normal distribution) doesn't apply. In other words, you'd be hard-pressed to find a guy whose voice lowered on the younger end of the curve, and it bothered him. All guys want their voices to change—unless they're a top performer in a boys' choir. And when it happens, boys are thrilled with the new resonance, and they enjoy hearing themselves.

There are, of course, two kinds of boys for whom this shift is traumatic: Those whose voices change late, and those who are in the midst of the change. Guys whose voices haven't begun dropping yet are often embarrassed by the way they sound when they talk. So it's not uncommon for these guys to talk less often because it's a constant reminder that they're "abnormal" (at least in their own thinking).

The universally common experience, of course, is the boy whose voice is in the midst of the transition between a boy's voice and a man's voice—between the upper registers and lower registers. Enter the voice break—that warbling sound that causes instant giggles from anyone within listening range. That cartoon character voice that sounds like a flip-flop between normalcy and falsetto.

Now, I wouldn't say that breast development for girls and vocal change for guys are equivalent. But they are similar in at least two ways.

First, this change can be massively diminishing to boys, making them feel awkward, broken, abnormal, weird, and embarrassed. But unlike girls and breasts, this period of change is relatively short-lived for guys.

A second similarity is how we, as caring parents, should respond. Moms, I'd encourage you to pretend as though you don't even notice the way a boy's voice sounds. Don't make comments such as, "Oh, that's so cute!" or even a dismissive "Oh, you'll be fine." Even though such statements are positively motivated, they become verifying statements to guys, confirming that everyone notices this horrible, awkward thing.

Dads can play a slightly different role. In general, ignoring voice breaks (especially in mixed company) is best. But since this is a universal experience for guys, it can be helpful to give an affirming comment to your son about how cool it is that his voice is changing. There's an art to knowing when this is appropriate and when it isn't.

But in general, make this kind of comment only when the relational environment is safe for the guy (in a one-on-one conversation with you). And don't say something if the boy doesn't indicate that he noticed it. But if he pauses or laughs at himself or gives some other indication that his voice break is on his radar, it can be good to offer an affirming, normalizing comment. Single moms, you might find (as you do in so many areas) that you have to cautiously step into this dad-role. Again, don't make too big a deal of it; just toss in a casual, affirming, normalizing comment in a moment when your son gives indication that he's aware of this change.

Menstruation and Nocturnal Emission
Okay, here we go.

If this were a book *for* middle schoolers, this would be the second section they'd turn to, right after the part about breast size and penis length. Oddly enough, as a parent it's probably one of the *last* parts you want to read. But stick with me for a moment.

In educational theory, there's this idea called "the null curriculum." It's the stuff we either never talk about or avoid talking about. And the idea is that our null curriculum teaches students a lot. For example, if we never talk about homosexuality, we inadvertently communicate that we have nothing to say on the topic, that God has nothing to say about the topic, and that kids should merely go along with whatever information they hear from other sources in their lives.

The same holds true for these highly personal subjects of menstruation and nocturnal emissions. When we don't talk about them, we compound middle schoolers' notions that they're bad or dirty or wrong. Therefore, we have to talk to our students about periods and wet dreams, to end the myth that they're bad or dirty or wrong. Each is a beautiful part of God's brilliant design—even though we sometimes treat them as parts of the fall, rather than parts of creation.

Both menstruation and nocturnal emissions are, at least in the public consciousness, understood as physical markers that puberty is happening. This is especially true with menstruation. Developmental experts usually refer to breast bud development as the first physical marker of puberty in girls; and many girls are well into puberty before their first period. But the marker remains strong.

It's almost like those time estimates from Google Maps or Map-Quest that say how long it'll take to get to a particular city. We might not even know whether the predicted travel time is to the city limits or to the city center. (It's to the city center, by the way.) So when we get to the city limits, we start thinking, *Well, we're kinda here*. But when we get to the city center, we *know* we've arrived. The same is true with a girl's first period or a guy's first wet dream. There are plenty of indications that kids have entered puberty prior to those physical events (they're already within the city limits), but those markers make it exceedingly clear that puberty has arrived.

So, menstruation. You all know this, right? You know that (just making sure dads understand, here) a period is the natural release of the uterine lining (and accompanying blood) at the end of the monthly fertility cycle. It's usually from three to five days long, but anywhere from two to seven days is still considered a normal length. During menstruation, it's common for women (and girls) to experience loads of unpleasant physical and emotional side effects, including cramping in the uterus, abdominal pain, headaches, depression and emotionality, feeling "bloated" (which is due to premenstrual water retention), and a host of other not-so-fun realities. The severity of these side effects varies from woman to woman, and from period to period.[2]

And, of course, the reason menstruation is tied to puberty is because puberty brings fertility. Menstruation is the physical sign that a girl's body is now pregnancy-ready. (By the way, *menstruation* is the name of the process, *menses* is the correct name for an individual cycle, and *period* is the colloquialism for menses.)

There are lots of middle school parenting implications of menstruation, although they're mostly for the moms:

- On overnight trips always bring along an extra starter pad or two, or send them with your daughter if you're not there. Remember, most young teen girls don't use tampons at first, so pads are the way to go. There's nothing worse than a girl being at summer camp and having her first period when no one is prepared to help her.

- Talk to your daughter about her period. She'll likely get some of this information during their health class at school, but it's more important that it come from you (mom). Again, normalize it—create a safe environment to talk about this normal and good part of being a woman. (Ha! I'm sure some of you women reading this right now are thinking, Good?)

- Single dads, you have a special challenge on this one. If you have a particularly open and honest conversational relationship with your daughter, it's possible you could talk about it with her. But she still needs an adult woman to give her more information (particularly, some of the details of personal care). If your daughter is part of a church youth group, see if there's a female adult leader who would be willing to have this conversation with her—or maybe an aunt or other caring adult female friend who can be both nonchalant (normalizing) and specific.

Whether you talk with your daughter yourself (moms) or find a female friend or relative who will speak with her (single dads), go out of your way to make sure your daughter has a trusted adult she can talk with privately, someone she can come to with any questions or concerns.

Okay, so, on to wet dreams! (Are we having fun yet?)

Nocturnal emissions (also known as "wet dreams" or "spontaneous orgasms") seem to be discussed even less frequently than menstruation. Maybe that's because girls have to do something about their periods, so parents are—in a sense—forced to engage. But there's not much that needs to be done about wet dreams, so we stay silent. And this silence creates all kinds of confusion for boys. It's that "null curriculum" I mentioned earlier—our lack of conversation about this topic teaches more than we realize or are willing to admit.

First, let's talk about the technical stuff. Nocturnal emission is the spontaneous ejaculation of semen while sleeping. It's often, though not always, accompanied by an erotic dream. It sometimes results in waking up, but not always. It's usually accompanied by a tingling sensation, which, for many young teen boys, feels akin to urinating. (This is why they'll often wake up the first few times and believe they've wet their beds.) For men (and post-pubescent young teen guys), semen buildup is a continual process. So nocturnal emission is the body's way (read: God's design) to release the excess semen.

I'll say this plainly: Most of us in the church have lingering baggage about wet dreams being somehow sinful. This may be a holdover from Jewish purity laws. Or maybe it's a holdover from Augustine's belief that nocturnal emission is connected to a lustful mind. (He referred to it as "the glue of lust," an unfortunately vivid description, to be sure.) Or, more likely, it's the reality of those oft-accompanying erotic dreams, which we'd like to believe are "controllable."

But the reality is that a teenage guy can no more control whether or not he has wet dreams than he can control his changing voice or growing taller. Wet dreams are just part of the package, so to speak. The only guys who don't have many wet dreams are those who regularly find another means of releasing excess semen, through sex or masturbation (which we'll talk about in a bit).

Moms, since it's not appropriate for you to talk to your sons about this stuff, please make sure your husband chats about this with your son, or that there's another man in his life (a youth group leader, caring relative, or family friend) who has this conversation with your son.

Dads, don't let this be part of your null curriculum. I'm continually amazed by the lack of information and total confusion middle school guys have about this subject—not to mention guilt and embarrassment. Just recently, one of my small group guys said, "Oh, yeah, that's when you pee in your sleep." And another guy responded, "No, it's not pee! It's your baby-makin' stuff, and it happens because you have a dirty mind!"

Here's a practical rule: If your young teen boy wants to wash his own sheets (a common practice, born out of embarrassment), let him. And don't make a big deal about it. (Although having dad mention to the boy that these dreams are a normal part of becoming a man can be helpful, too.)

Oh, and we can't forget about spontaneous erections. This subject became a topic of discussion at my guys' small group recently. (First, I was going to say the subject "came up," and then "arose." I find I'm tiptoeing all through this section—every phrase I write sounds like a double entendre. I can just hear my middle school guys giggling!) I was a little surprised by how my guys were willing and able to talk about this experience. It was as if we'd tapped into a little safe zone where they finally felt they could share their awkwardness.

Let me pause here to offer a teaching point for the moms. Please understand that spontaneous erections are just part of being a teenage guy, and they don't always happen because a guy is thinking about sex. Spontaneous erections are quite frustrating to almost every guy. And, man alive, the fear of being "discovered" or having to stand in front of a group while having one is sheer horror. So many things can cause spontaneous erections, and often the source is not obvious to the middle school guy.

Back to the story: All the guys started sharing how annoying it is, how they bend over at their school desks (hoping to stay anonymous), how they decline being called out, how they make up lies to cover why they can't stand up. One guy said, "We have to wear these shorts in gym class, and they kill me! Every time we run, I get a boner! It's horrible. I have to tuck 'it' between my legs and just keep running!" (This brought out shrieks of "Isn't that painful?" and "I know what you mean!" from the other guys.)

Two parenting implications here that should be obvious:

1. Dads, talk about this with your son. Every boy has (or will have) this experience, and they all wonder if they're freaks or if there's something wrong with their penises or if they're just overly dirty. Help them understand that it's normal, it's part of the changes they're going through, and the frequency of them will subside over time. Moms, make sure you have a man (your husband, ideally, but another caring man who already knows your son can step in) who is willing to talk about this

stuff with your son. (It will *seriously freak them out* if you talk to them about it.)

2. Just as you should give a girl who might be dealing with menstrual pain some space and the permission to opt out of activities, be sensitive to your son as well. If he says he doesn't want to stand up—don't make him. Just let the moment pass on by.

Masturbation

This is an extremely challenging section to write, and I expect some readers won't agree with my comments. For that reason, I strongly encourage you to do more reading from other sources (both those you trust and those whose perspectives are different than your own).

Let's start with this: The subject of masturbation is very different for guys than it is for girls. But there are definitely some aspects of this discussion relevant to both genders.

First, the social acceptance of masturbation has shifted in the last 20 years. What was once seen as a somewhat taboo practice (even in the locker-room talk of guys) is now considered normal. Morning drive radio DJs talk about "rubbing one out." And didn't everything change once *Seinfeld* aired that episode about "being the master of your domain"? Suddenly, almost with a collective national sigh, it was normal and okay to talk about this previously closeted activity. This also means that the even-more taboo subject (and practice) of girls masturbating has become culturally normative.

Another factor that has implications for both genders is the increased access to pornography in this Internet age. There are still young teens who haven't been exposed to porn, but they're the exception, rather than the rule. Even "good, churched kids" with an active faith and engaged parents have been exposed to more porn, and significantly more *graphic* porn, than most of us adults were at their age. This adds both to the "normalcy" of masturbation and to the urge. (It's almost impossible for a teenage guy to view porn and not get an erection.) And I know both from studies and experience that even the most quickly viewed graphic images can get locked into our memories to be easily retrieved at a later time—whether they're welcome or not.

One more commonality between guys and girls: Masturbation often starts, for young teens, as experimentation and getting to know their suddenly foreign bodies. If kids are willing to talk about this, they'll usually admit that their first attempts at masturbation were more about discovering what was and wasn't possible, about feeling new things, about checking out the plumbing.

But here's where the parallel tracks for the genders begin to part ways, at least from my perspective. Guys—with their constant buildup of semen, brains that are more naturally attuned to think about sex on a regular basis (as opposed to intimacy, which is more the line of thinking, daydreaming, and longing for girls), and the constant fear of spontaneous erections—have a more urgent physiological "need" for the release that comes from masturbation, wet dreams, or—hopefully not for many young teens—actual sexual encounters. (I've talked to boys who've been so sexually active as young teens that they had no use or need for masturbation.)

There's a fine line here, and we all know this. Masturbation can easily (and often, for guys and girls alike) become an obsession, something that rules them. And it can often become inseparably linked to other practices of the mind, such as viewing porn and fantasizing, that are horribly destructive to their sexual identity development, relational development, and faith development.

Yet even conservative family author, radio host, and psychologist Dr. James Dobson talks about masturbation among adolescents as a normal activity that's not harmful in moderation: "It is my opinion that masturbation is not much of an issue with God. It's a normal part of adolescence, which involves no one else…if you do [masturbate], it is my opinion that you should not struggle with guilt over it."[3]

My experience with middle school guys tells me that the boy who "never, ever" masturbates is a mythical creature. And those boys who tell you otherwise are likely lying. They might feel massive guilt about it, and their guilt might decrease the frequency; but they still masturbate.

It seems weird to talk about masturbation in terms like "all good things in moderation." But there's a sense in which this is true. For boys, masturbation, in moderation, is part of the growing-up experience. Masturbation, in moderation, can actually help guys spend less time obsessing and fantasizing about sex because it releases built-up sexual pressure.

This topic is challenging for even the most engaged parent to talk about because the line between helpful and "in moderation" on one end and obsessive and "fueled by lust" on the other end is extremely difficult to nail down.

So, let's leave it at this for now:

- Masturbation, for guys, is a normal part of the adolescent experience. We need to talk about it in sensitive and spiritually appropriate ways (and, again, this is same-gender parent discussion stuff—single parents will need to find a same-gendered stand-in).
- Masturbation, for girls, is becoming a normal part of the adolescent experience, due to shifting cultural norms and messages. Moms need to help their daughters think about what they're really longing for.
- Masturbation for both genders can quickly and easily become a destructive obsession, especially when fueled by porn, and we need to talk about this also, offering them examples of lives ruined by porn and obsessive sexual behavior.[4]

Okay, so that was a touchy subject. (C'mon, I had to slip in just one double entendre!)

Period Parties and Rites of Passage

Remember, adolescence is a *recent* cultural phenomenon. And also remember that it was only about 100 years ago that the term came into popular use. Before that time, the shift from childhood to young adulthood didn't have the ever-widening "holding period" we provide today.[5]

In fact, throughout most of history, the shift from childhood to young adulthood *appeared* to occur at a single point in time (although reality was more gradual, of course). And—get this—

almost every culture around the globe (historically speaking, that is) had some kind of ceremony or marker to acknowledge this transition. Often referred to as a "rite of passage," these family or community acknowledgments have almost completely faded away. We see remnants of them in the Jewish bar mitzvah and bat mitzvah[6] (rites of passage and inclusion into the world of adults for boys and girls, respectively), the Latin Quinceañera[7] (a girl's fifteenth birthday party that traditionally marks her "coming out" as a young woman), the practice of Native American boys going on a "spirit quest," and even the debutante balls of the moneyed American South.

Yet the only rites of passage observed by most North American families these days are less about pomp-and-circumstance and celebrating the teenager than they are about giving the young person some new permission:

- Getting a driver's license (around 16 years old in most states)
- Graduating from high school (at approximately 18 years)
- Gaining the right to vote (at 18 years)
- Gaining the legal right to possess alcohol (at 21 years)

It's interesting that these new "rites" are not only about permission, but also tend to fall near the *end* of adolescence, rather than as a marker of puberty—when rites of passage have traditionally occurred.[8]

Historically, rites of passage were (and remain, in some subcultures) public spectacles of rejoicing, honoring the young subjects, and welcoming them as fully identified members of the community. In many cultures, a girl's first period was cause for great celebration. It signaled the coming of age and birthing-readiness of the young woman, and this was cause for celebration because fertility was critical to the future existence of the people group. The tribe would gather together and honor the newly fertile young woman (perhaps for the only time in an otherwise male-dominated culture). She'd be acknowledged as no longer a child but a woman—and with all the privileges (and responsibilities) due a woman in their culture.

I don't know about you, but I haven't been to a good period party in years.[9] Actually, this isn't wholly true. In my home, we had a period party, of sorts, for my daughter (not that we *called* it that!). My wife and I (mostly my wife) had already talked with our daughter about all the changes her body was going through. But when she had her first period, we decided to mark this transition point in her life with a celebration of who she was becoming. We took her out of school for a day, let her get a new haircut and a manicure (something she'd been begging for), had a masseuse come to our home to give her a private massage, and had a special family dinner, complete with gifts. My son, Max (then about nine), was a little confused by the whole thing. But Liesl felt like a princess. My wife also planned a small gathering of women whom Liesl had chosen because they were the kind of women she wanted to be like. They gathered for a women-only tea where they offered words of blessing to Liesl and spoke together about what it means to be a woman.

There's been a small resurgence of interest in rites of passage in both the Christian community and the North American culture at large, and a number of helpful books and articles are readily available.[10] I highly affirm this trend and strongly encourage you as a parent to think about how you can plan a meaningful rite of passage for your son or daughter. Since adolescence sprawls in front of young teens as a more-than-a-decade-long span of transition, current rites of passage aren't about saying, "You're now an adult." Instead, they're more about acknowledging that the young teen is now *on the road* to adulthood. Good stuff.

About the Shifting Age of Puberty

In chapter 1, I wrote a tiny bit about the plunging average age in the onset of puberty. Really, it's such a fascinating change.[11]

To recap briefly: In the early 1900s, the average age for the onset of puberty (in girls) was about 14 and one-half years old. By the 1970s, this average had dropped to somewhere around 13 years old. And over the past several decades, the average age for the onset of puberty has continued to drop. The most recent research shows puberty begins around 11 years old on average in the United States. Some studies say the overall average is as young as 10.5—with the average age among African-American and Latino girls as much as a full year younger.

Why has this happened? For years, there were three competing theories:

- Some proposed the drop in puberty age was due to diet and, more specifically, the increasing amount of additives and preservatives in the average American diet.
- Others agreed that the drop was diet-related, but proposed, conversely, that it was because today's young people have a *better* and *more well-rounded diet.*
- Still others suggested the shift was a physiological response to the cultural expectation that kids act older at younger ages.

I believed, and taught in seminars, that the reason was some combination of the three. However, in more recent years, research (and common opinion among developmental specialists) has firmly landed on the first notion.

So preservatives and additives in our diet have brought on this shift. But here's the really weird thing: Even in cultures where the diet does *not* include modified food, there's still been a drop in the onset of puberty—not as drastic a drop, but a drop nonetheless. And no one has a good explanation for this. It's also not clear if this trend would reverse if we began to eat food that was entirely free of preservatives and additives. Certainly, there still seems to be a cultural component at work.

The church has—in large part—been oddly resistant to acknowledge this shift in the age of onset for puberty.[12] I believe much of this resistance is well intentioned (even though it lends itself to a bit of the proverbial ostrich-head-in-the-sand syndrome). Churches, and engaged parents in general, have wanted to protect their kids from rushing into adolescent behaviors that are beyond their maturity. But to disavow the shift, or somehow believe we can change it, is to discard the opportunity for age-appropriate parenting.

We simply cannot deny that adolescence now begins around 11 years old. We must be responsive to the real-world and body experiences of our 11- and 12-year-olds, rather than waiting until they are 13 or 14 to address what they are going through.

Certainly, this lowered-age thing brings up all kinds of new complications, which we'll get into a bit more in future chapters. For example, what does it mean for an 11-year-old girl who's slightly ahead of the curve (in terms of her physical development) to be ogled by her male peers and adult men? She has 11 years of life experience and a barely usable third-person perspective.

In my opinion, the lowering of the average age of puberty greatly compounds the reasons why intentional, engaged parenting is so crucial, and why it's a make-or-break time in the psychological, emotional, relational, and spiritual development of a human being.

Restating Parenting Implications

I've tried to weave implications throughout this chapter, as I do throughout this entire book. My desire is for *Understanding Your Young Teen* to be all about implications, rather than a dissertation on development.

But I want to restate a few of the notions I've harped on multiple times already:

- The physical changes of early adolescence are truly massive and world changing. And they bring with them universal concern and fear. Every young teen feels abnormal at one point or another.
- Because of this universal concern and fear, young teens need caring adults (parents and others) who can walk with them through this turbulent change, who are affirming and willing to talk, who will answer their questions without inducing guilt, and who can help them feel normal.
- Helping young teens feel normal (and even good) is one of the most important aspects of effective parenting.
- Great middle school parenting calls for courage because it's awkward to talk about lots of this stuff.

A FEW WORDS TO PARENTS

THE (SEX) TALK

There's no doubt, most parents love their kids. We spend money, time, and energy on them. We navigate the stages of their growing up, and try to teach them everything we can. But unfortunately many parents bail out on their kids regarding one critical part of growing up: The minefield of sexuality. When is the last time you've talked with your kids about something related to sexuality or dating?

Research says that a majority of the parents of young teens report that they've talked to their child about sex and sexuality. And yet, a minority of young teens will say their parents have talked to them about it. On behalf of middle schoolers (and middle school youth workers) everywhere, I beg you not to be a parent who shies away from conversations about sex, boyfriends and girlfriends, and intimacy, no matter how intimidating it feels, because research also says that "Teens who talk to their parents about sex are more likely to delay their first sexual encounter…" (*Time,* December 7, 2009).

Often, we parents want to believe that our middle school son/daughter is still an innocent child, and our role is to protect that innocence. But the truth is that they are becoming young men and women, and their naiveté is slowing disappearing. It's crucial for us to face that reality, so that we can serve and help our kids.

In our family, we've told our sons we want them to know what's real, and not have to guess about what's true or not. We try to initiate conversations with them so they don't get confused about facts, and about God's design for sexuality. Even though there have been moments of clumsiness, our sons have appreciated our attempt at openness.

Some of you might agree with the concept, but think "I have NO idea how to tackle that stuff with a middle schooler, because my own parents never approached conversations like that!" Here are a few tips to help get you started:

A guarantee: The first conversation (and maybe all of them) is going to be awkward, at least a little bit. You're not going to know exactly what to say. But that's okay! Find a good book/resource to read first, and be prepared: know where to go for answers.

Realize that your son or daughter doesn't need "The Talk"—kids need ongoing conversations about most everything related to sexuality. Don't avoid asking a question because you think it might lead to an uncomfortable and potentially embarrassing conversation!

Play detective: Look for good windows of time to bring up the conversation. Have conservations on their terms...when it's convenient for them, not you (for example, riding in the car is convenient for them; when they're in the middle of homework is not).

Start small: Watch TV with your kids, and then talk to them about topics that come up. Ask them about their favorite websites, movies, songs (and lyrics), or video games and be genuinely interested. Consider putting your family's home computer in a "high-traffic area" of your house to allow you opportunities for conversations to happen more naturally.

You've already made a huge investment in your son or daughter. Don't bail out on your young teen when it comes to helping him or her navigate the realm of sexuality, no matter how awkward it feels for you (and them).

—Scott Rubin is the junior high pastor
at Willow Creek Church in South Barrington, Illinois.

Chapter 4

Mind-Warp
(Cognitive Development)

One Sunday morning I was teaching on God's forgiveness in my church's middle school ministry. Partway through the teaching time, I used a few mini case studies to check for understanding.[1] I read a short blip that went something like this:

> Charlotte is a committed follower of Jesus, and she usually makes decisions that reflect that desire. But she also wants to be popular. Last weekend, Charlotte got invited to a party with a bunch of cool kids from school. And, uncertain about how to act in this setting, Charlotte ended up having some alcoholic drinks. Now Charlotte has tons of guilt. She feels like Jesus could never forgive her and that she must not be a Christian anymore.

I asked the kids what they'd say to Charlotte if she confided her feelings to them. Hands went up.

The first kid I called on said, "I'd tell her alcohol is stupid!"

Okay.

I tried another student who said, "I'd say, 'Jesus still loves you, but it's too bad you're not a Christian anymore.'"

Uh...

The girl in the front row was thrusting her hand in the air and making an "ooh, ooh, ooh!" sound. I reluctantly asked her what she'd say to Charlotte. With a huge grin and a basketful of confidence, she responded, "I'd tell her that my name is Charlotte, too!"

I believe my face fell a bit. Finally, the pastor's daughter raised her hand with a look on her face that said, *I'll help you out here, Marko; I know what you're looking for.*

"Bethany?" I pleaded. With a bored voice that simultaneously mocked both her fellow youth groupers and me, she flatly sighed and said, "I'd tell her Jesus forgives her."

Whew. At least *someone* got it.

Ah, the minds of middle schoolers. It's the combination of their innocence and their willingness to verbalize just about any thought that makes engagement with middle schoolers such a wild ride at times.

Stage Theory

We spent the previous chapter talking about the many physical changes early adolescents experience in their bodies. While these are the most visible changes and tend to be the ones people focus on, I don't believe they're the *most* significant changes of the young teen years. I've found that the shift in thinking that occurs during the middle school years is even more significant, particularly when we consider the parenting implications. Cognitive change has an enormous impact on all the other areas of change in the life of a young teen (all the chapters on development that follow this one). It really is, in simple terms, the determining factor that separates children from young adults.

In the early 1920s, a Swiss dude named Jean Piaget proposed a theory that suggested that children go through a series of different developmental stages in terms of how their brains process and understand information.[2] Piaget's theory of cognitive development has been widely tested and accepted over the years,[3] and his research has been the foundation built upon by numerous other scholars in related fields.[4]

When it comes to parenting young teens, it's the final two stages of Piaget's congitive theory that need our consideration. Piaget refers to those final stages of cognitive development as "Concrete Operations" and "Formal Operations." Or, in lay terms, concrete thinking and abstract thinking.

Concrete thinking results in a rigid, black-and-white understanding of the world. A world without nuance or paradox. We can readily see this in preteens, right? They have a wonderfully "concluded" worldview, with their little systematic theologies all worked out and their worldview encased in plastic wrap. Ten-year-olds have a confidence in their opinions born out of a general, limited belief that everyone sees the world and everything in it just as they do. Preteen thinking is concrete, linear, pragmatic, tangible, and simplistic. But puberty really messes that up, just like the mother eagle that stirs up the nest in order to prepare her eaglet for learning how to fly (Deuteronomy 32:11).

Around the onset of puberty, the brain begins a transition in how it processes information. This brings on a long trek into useable abstract thinking. This journey is far from completed during the middle school years. In fact, some research shows that adolescents are postponing the use of abstract thinking well into their teen years, and often well into their twenties.[5]

I like to view abstract thinking as God's "puberty gift" to young teens. If they *did* have period parties, God would show up with a card with this message written inside: I LOVE YOU, AND I'M PROUD OF YOU. AS A PRESENT, I'M GOING TO CHANGE YOUR ENTIRE WORLD BY BLESSING YOU WITH THE GIFT OF ABSTRACT THOUGHT. HAPPY PUBERTY!

The change doesn't happen overnight, of course. It's not as if they're concrete thinkers one day and abstract thinkers the next. The change is gradual, and young teens slowly start to bump in and out of abstract thinking. If one could measure a teenager's use of abstract thought over a period of years, progress would be seen. But in everyday life, the experience is much more hit or miss.

Thumbs Up

Now, abstract thinking isn't a muscle, of course. But being a visual guy, I find it helpful to envision it that way. Abstract thinking is like a brand-new muscle kids receive when they're young teens. But it's undeveloped, and they have no idea how to use it.

I had a bad run of thumb injuries in late adolescence. As a high school junior, I worked as a dishwasher in a Chinese restaurant. But

I'd often help with food prep also. As such, I was usually the guy who had to chop the cabbage. We'd take a large crate of cabbage and, using a cleaver and butcher block, whack it into quarters, which could then be fed through a massive food shredder. One time, I made the mistake of challenging the cook to a race to see who could quarter a case of cabbage heads first. In hindsight, I can see how this was a race to be lost.

When attacking one particularly large cabbage head, the cleaver didn't go all the way through, and I tried to yank it back out. Fearful of the extremely sharp blade as it came flying out, I reacted by bringing it quickly back down—on my thumb.

Luckily, I didn't chop off my thumb. But I cut all the way to the bone, between the knuckle and the rest of my hand. And worse, I cut my tendon in half.

A few days later, a hand surgeon stretched what looked like a bloody rubber band out from my thumb and said, "This is your tendon!" I remember feeling the tug and responding, "Great, please put it back in my thumb."

Internal and external stitches followed, as did a plaster mold around my thumb and extending all the way up to my elbow, which was held up by a sling. For six weeks I had my hand in a constant "thumbs up" position. I felt like a dork.

Two years later, as a college freshman, I was working in a pizza joint, slicing mozzarella on a circular meat slicer. Wicked sharp things, those meat slicers. So when the tip of my thumb got too close, I lost it—right at the edge of, and a little into, my thumbnail. A few days later I had a skin graft taken from my inner hip and sewed onto my thumb tip.[6] Repeat: Plaster mold around my thumb and all the way up to my elbow. Repeat: Sling. Repeat: Six weeks in a thumbs-up position. ("I'm doin' great! How you doin'?")

In both of those situations, my thumb was immobilized for six weeks. In both of those situations, I had the same experience at the end of the six weeks: The doctor removed the splint, wiggled my thumb, checked out a few things, and said, "Everything's great. You're good to go."

And in both cases, I held my newly freed "thumbs up" thumb in front of my face and stared at it. I commenced sending massive quantities of brain signals down through my arm and directly to the muscles in my thumb, commanding it to MOVE! But it wouldn't move. Not one little tiny bit. "Everything was great," but I had no muscle memory of how to use it. My thumb had no recent history of movement, and it had atrophied.

Later that day, I could wiggle my thumb a tiny bit. After a few days, I had about half the full range of motion. And after about a week, all was normal.

These thumb experiences have stayed close to me over the years because they're such great snapshots of what's going on with young teens and their new abstract thinking ability. They have it—they're theoretically capable of formal operational thinking. But it's a foreign land of the unknown. They have no idea how to use it, no experience of the process, no "muscle memory" of how.

What Is Abstract Thought?

Abstract thought can be described, perhaps in an overly simplistic way, as *thinking about thinking*. In more expanded terms, abstract thinking includes the abilities to consider—

* Third-person perspective
* Self-awareness
* Nuance and gray areas
* Paradox
* Systems
* Speculation and inference

But what does this mean for a young teen with a newly acquired abstract thinking ability? Most of us (as adults) have been utilizing abstract thinking for so long that it's easy to forget what it's like not to have this ability or at least not to have it function well. I can't overemphasize how important it is for parents of middle schoolers to understand this stuff.

Hypothesizing and Speculating

Abstract thinking allows teenagers (and adults, of course) to create multiple scenarios—real or imaginary—of "what might be." Teenagers are just beginning to consider likely (and unlikely) down-the-line results of various actions and choices—both their own and others'. Of course, they're also really bad at doing this because it's a new ability. But they have the basic cognitive tools to do it.[7]

Speculating is directly tied to decision making and is the practice of thinking through likely outcomes. We adults do this quickly (most of the time) and intuitively. When presented with a choice, we immediately (again, in most cases) speculate about the likely outcomes of the various options. We might call this "making an informed decision." Again, children and preteens aren't capable of making this kind of informed decision, as they don't possess the ability to speculate.

Empathizing

I live near Tijuana, Mexico, which is an area filled with poverty. If I take my two children to visit families who live in a Tijuana garbage dump and scavenge for food and sustenance, then my children would most likely have two very different experiences. Max, my still prepubescent 12-year-old—a naturally sensitive boy—would experience deep sympathy for the children and families he encounters. He'll feel bad for them and want to help. However, Liesl, my 16-year-old daughter, will likely experience empathy. She'll also feel bad for the children, but she'll take it a step further. She'll empathize as she imagines (even "feels") what life would be like for an impoverished child. She'll place herself in a child's shoes and perceive life from the child's perspective, a perspective that's completely third person and outside herself. Liesl might also wrestle with abstract questions, such as, "Why was this child born in this place and to this poverty? And why was I born into the comfortable life that I have?"

Doubting

Doubting, of course, occurs when we internally question our own beliefs. This is a very abstract thought process, and it's not possible prior to adolescence. But it's absolutely essential to faith development and a wonderful developmental gift in God's design (much more about this in chapter 8).

Self-Perceiving

Preteens don't have the ability to think of themselves beyond what they see in the mirror or what others say about them. But abstract thinking brings the ability to think about oneself and speculate about how one might be perceived from another's perspective. Once again, teenagers—especially younger ones—are notoriously bad at this. They often incorrectly perceive how others see them—or assume everyone is "checking them out."[8]

Emoting

Emotions are abstract. And since children don't think abstractly, they're significantly limited in their emotional options. Of course, young teens often *express* emotions with great verve; but they're deeply limited in their ability to *understand* and *interpret* emotions, both in themselves, and, especially, in others. (We'll focus more fully on this in the next chapter.)

Identity Formation?

It would be wrong to say that identity formation *begins* in adolescence. Our identities are being formed from Day One. All the messages we take in from family, friends, the culture at large, and—hopefully—the Word of God, shape our self-perception. The shift that occurs during adolescence—thanks to our friend, abstract thinking—is that young teens acquire the ability to take charge of their own identity formation. Since they gain self-perception (and all the other outcomes we've just discussed), they can begin to actively direct the course of their identity formation. They make choices and see the implications of who they are and who they're becoming. They begin speculating about who they want to be, not only in regard to what careers they'd like to pursue someday, but also what kind of people they want to be—and what kind of people they want *others* to identify them as being. In other words, adolescence provides the opportunity to choose who one becomes.

An example of this: I was talking, just weeks ago, with my seventh-grade guys, in our small group, about what kind of people they want to be when they're adults. I started by asking them all to share what jobs they'd dreamed about having when they were little kids. ("Fireman," "Professional Gamer," and the like). Then I asked each one to share what job or career he could imagine in his future now ("Youth Pastor," "Professional Gamer," and so on).

Then I said, "Now I want you to think about what kind of man you want to be. I'm not talking about what you do, but about who you are. If you die when you're 32, what would you want people to say about your character?" Then I asked them to think for a minute, in silence.

The whole (hyper) tone of our time shifted, and it became one of those rare (holy) moments when the guys were 100 percent engaged. Quietly, and with an almost reverent tone, they each shared a few thoughts that blew me away, and sustained me through weeks of unruliness that followed.

"I think I have the ability to be a leader, and I want to be a leader who isn't a jerk, but leads with humility."

"I make people laugh a lot; but I want to be more than that. I want to be someone who brings life to relationships and groups of people."

"I want to be someone who is known for his integrity. Oh, and I think I have more leadership in me than I've lived at this point in my life."

"I want to be a professional gamer." (See, one was still stuck at a concrete level of thinking.)

All this points to the reason identity development is such a major task in adolescence. The reality is that by the time an adolescent reaches her mid-twenties, her identity will be mostly formed. (And, remember, this is the whole point of culture giving teenagers a respite between childhood and adulthood.) Sure, we all continue to shape and refine our identities throughout adulthood, but the core formation work is done. The course is mostly set. And that's why it's so important to help our young teens get headed in the right direction.

Two Stories

Since this is such an important issue for parents to understand, I'd like to tell a couple of stories to help flesh it out a bit. First, a story about concrete thinking; then a story about abstract thinking.

A friend of mine was speaking at a camp for middle school kids. Central to the recreational offerings of the camp was a pond the kids could swim in. On one side of the pond stood a two-stories-high tower, and suspended on a cable stretched across the middle of the pond was a trapeze. The challenge was to climb the tower, jump out over the pond, and try to grab the trapeze. If one succeeded, the reward was a few moments of hanging there, as well as some cheers from those watching. Of course, those successful jumps weren't nearly as interesting as the gnarly misses that resulted in sideways two-story drops into the pond. That's what everyone was really hoping to see.

Many of the middle schoolers at the camp found this little test of courage to be the coolest thing they'd ever experienced. But, as you might guess, many others would have nothing to do with it and stayed well away from the tower's ladder.

Late in the week, my friend had been asked to share the gospel and offer kids an opportunity to respond. At one point in her talk, she was trying to describe what it meant to "take a leap of faith." As a seasoned middle school youth worker, she was well aware of the fact that this is a very abstract concept that would be tough for kids to grasp. So she wanted to find a way—on the fly—to illustrate the idea. The tower and trapeze sprang to mind (a great concrete example). She explained that taking a leap of faith is kind of like jumping off the tower down at the pond. "It's a little scary. You're not completely sure what's going to happen or what grabbing that trapeze is going to be like—but you jump."

(Just as a side note: I'm not sure my friend realized it at the time, but another way this metaphor works is how kids who were "into" the tower jump often did it over and over again, just like how middle schoolers often believe they need to "become a Christian" over and over again, typically when they're at camp.)

After the meeting time was over, an incoming sixth-grade girl approached my friend. She was shy, and she held back until the other students had walked away. Then she said, "I have a problem. I think I want to do what you talked about—become a 'follower of Jesus.' But I'm way too afraid to jump off that tower."

At this point my friend thought the girl was speaking metaphorically—that she meant she was afraid to take a "leap of faith." But the girl continued, "Do I *really* have to jump off the pond tower if I want to become a Christian?"

Ah! This wonderful little concrete thinker had completely missed the metaphorical nature of the illustration, which is ironic since that image was my friend's attempt to make an abstract idea more concrete. But this sixth grader thought she had to jump off the tower by the pond in order to follow Jesus.

So they took her down to the pond and threw her off the tower. (I'm kidding!)

This is a great example of a preteen thinking in *very* concrete ways. It's an extreme example, in many ways, as many preteens—even those utilizing concrete thinking—would still catch the metaphor in that example. But this is the kind of thinking many middle schoolers are locked into—especially when they think about subjects that are truly abstract (such as taking a leap of faith).

This second story shows the other extreme.

I took a group of middle school kids to Mexico on a short-term mission trip. We stayed at and worked with an orphanage and one of the local churches connected with it. During the trip our students were involved in four tasks: Helping around the orphanage, building a few small houses for people in the community, running a "kids club" (like a Vacation Bible School) for children in the community, and going into the community with members of the church to talk to people. This last task was, by far, the most intimidating one for most of our kids.

We'd prepared our middle schoolers for months, and we urged them to take a backseat in the conversations, especially since they had to rely on a translator. But the discussions often centered on why these American teenagers were in their community, which often led to spiritual discussions. We were careful not to build an expectation of lots of "conversions," but we wanted to work alongside the members of this church in their efforts to reach out to their local community.

One student on the trip was an eighth-grade guy named Garrett. He'd been reasonably active in our middle school group for a couple of years, but he seemed to be one of those kids who kind of blends into the crowd. He hadn't shown any particularly elevated leadership ability or even much spiritual interest—prior to this trip.

But while we were in Mexico, it became obvious to all of us that Garrett had the spiritual gift of evangelism. While the other middle schoolers nervously avoided this face-to-face ministry, Garrett was never found on the construction sites or at the kids club. He was always grabbing a translator and someone from the church, walking around the community, and, in a beautifully innocent way, leading people to Christ. The small congregation we were working with more than doubled in size during the week we were there, and all the adults could see that it was largely because God was doing something pretty amazing through this middle school kid.

When we returned home, we had an opportunity to give a report to our congregation during a church service. Now, if your church's middle school ministry is anything like the ones I've been a part of, much of the communication with the church at large comes in the form of a request ("Please, we need more leaders!") or an apology ("We're sorry about that stain; we know blood is difficult to get out of carpeting, especially when it's mixed with eggs and marshmallow cream."). So—I'll admit—I saw this as an opportunity to score some points for our middle school ministry. (I have a tendency toward manipulation—but all for the glory of God, of course!)

I know my motives weren't completely pure. But I had these visions of Garrett sharing and all the blue-hairs in the church thinking, *Oh, what a wonderful boy! Our middle school ministry must be wonderful! Let's double their budget!*

Yeah.

So when I asked Garrett to share as part of our trip report, I said, "Be sure to tell everyone how you led all those people to Christ."

I stood in front of the church and gave an overview of the trip, calling out a few highlights. Then I asked Garrett to talk. He stepped up to the mic, not the least bit nervous (more from being clueless than from being confident), and started talking. I was standing a few feet away from him with cartoon-style, budget-increase dollar signs cha-chinging where my eyes would normally be.

When Garrett got to the "rope 'em in and bring it home" part of the story, he paused. Then he said, "Marko wanted me to tell you how I led a whole bunch of people to Christ."

My smile stiffened, and I thought, *No! You're not supposed to tell them I told you to say that!*

He continued, "But that's not what really happened."

Now I was in full-blown panic and trying with everything in me not to show it. Thoughts flew through my head of yanking him off the stage before he could say something really stupid. I had absolutely no idea what Garrett might say next.

Garrett paused for what seemed like a few minutes (although it was probably a few seconds). He tilted his head sideways, like a puppy trying to figure something out. Then the thought hit him, and he went with it. With a big grin on his face, Garrett said, "What really happened was, God led a bunch of people to himself through me!"

I was stunned. I was thinking, *Dude! I barely understand that!* I started to wonder if I should ask Garrett to disciple me.

That flash of abstract thinking even caught Garrett by surprise. And it was a stunning moment of clarity on a deeply abstract spiritual plane.

You Never Know

So here's the challenge of understanding your young teen.

It would be nice if your child were simply the concrete-thinking tower girl or Garrett. Then at least you'd know which path to take when talking about abstract things.

Yeah, that would be nice. But it's not reality.

The reality is that every young teen pops in and out of abstract thinking. Sure, the younger ones (sixth graders) are more likely to think concretely nearly all the time. And yes, the older ones (eighth graders) are more likely to have some ability to grasp abstract ideas. But reality isn't that clean.

You never really know what your son or daughter is actually hearing when you talk about abstract stuff. (By the way, this pretty much includes all spiritual stuff.) Their abstract "thinking muscle" is so new and tiny that it's better to assume they aren't utilizing it and go the extra mile in seeking to concretize abstract stuff.

Good luck with that! I feel your pain.

Abstract Thought as a Gateway

I already wrote that I believe this cognitive shift is the change that has the biggest implications for parenting young teens. But that's not only because of the significance of the cognitive shift in and of itself and isolated from other implications. Instead, it's because all the issues we'll discuss in the next several chapters *flow out of* this brain shift.

Emotional development is directly tied to abstract thinking. Emotions are abstract. Children and preteens have limited emotional arsenals from which to draw because they're concrete thinkers. Abstract thinking opens up entire new vistas of emotional possibility and experience. (More on this in the next chapter.)

The massively changing relational landscape of early adolescence is also directly tied to abstract thinking. As young teens begin to think in new ways, they start to become more self-aware. This— along with other factors—brings about a shift in how kids form friendships and what's important to them in those friendships. (More about this in chapter 6.)

We all know that part of the teenage experience is gaining some independence. In fact, I've heard good parents encapsulate their roles as "helping our children become independent." This is a great perspective, and *all* young teens struggle, in one way or another, with this shift—as do most parents. (We'll talk about this more in chapter 7.)

Then, of course, there's spiritual change. Wow. This is the thing that keeps me passionate about middle schoolers. Every young teen is in the process of completely reinventing his or her worldview (no matter what that worldview is—Christian or otherwise). They're questioning the very things they've "concluded" in their preteen years and the things they've inherited from parents, churches, and other input. It's an extremely fragile and potent time of spiritual opportunity, and it's directly tied to the cognitive changes that are happening during their young teen years. (I'll address this, at length, in chapter 8.)

But before we move into those issues, let me say just a little more about the adolescent brain itself.

Other Brain Stuff

There's been a slew of new research on adolescent brain development in the last decade, revealing some fascinating stuff with huge implications for parenting.

For hundreds of years, the medical community assumed the human brain was fully developed in childhood. While it still needed more experience and data, it was thought that the raw goods were "all there." This was based mostly on the physical inspection of actual brains (both during surgery and postmortem).

But new advances in technology provided for real-time, non-invasive, three-dimensional brain scans of live brains. This provided an unprecedented opportunity for scientists to look at teenage brains *while still in* development. This book doesn't have space for a super-detailed investigation of all this (although reading more about it would be highly recommended).[9] But I'd like to provide a short overview, as it's captured quite a bit of my imagination in the last couple of years, and it's been the subject of lots of deep implication-oriented conversations among the middle school ministry peeps I hang with.

In short, the primary discovery is that the human brain isn't fully developed until the mid-twenties. There are three aspects of this I'd like to discuss a bit more:

Frontal Lobe Development

This is the biggie of this research and the component that's received the most attention. Real-time brain scans of teenagers have revealed that the frontal lobe (more formally called "the prefrontal cortex"), which is the part of the brain behind your forehead, is significantly underdeveloped in teenagers and isn't fully developed until the mid-twenties.

This critical discovery shines a light on many teenage behaviors. The frontal lobe is responsible for a bucket of astounding brain functions. Often called "the executive office" of the brain or the "decision-making center," the frontal lobe is responsible for processing things, such as—

- *Focus.* Teenagers have a hard time focusing on things without being distracted by everything else in the room.
- *Forethought.* Teenagers find it difficult to predict consequences to real or potential behavioral choices.
- *Impulse control.* Teenagers don't have a developed "governor" that helps moderate their impulses.
- *Organization.* Teenagers often do poorly at organizing tasks, time, relationships, and other things.
- *Planning.* Without this, we live in the here-and-now. It's hard for teens to make decisions based on what's coming in the future and the need to plan for it.
- *Judgment.* It's challenging for teenagers to discern the best choice in a particular situation, as they often don't possess a fully developed ability to make good judgment calls.
- *Empathy.* Teenagers struggle to see how their choices might impact others, as well as seeing something from another person's point of view (a distinctly abstract thinking ability). You

might notice that some of these frontal lobe functions are directly connected to the development of abstract thinking we discussed earlier.

- *Insight.* Teenagers have difficulty speculating about other peoples' behaviors and motivations and often draw wrong conclusions (as if this is something we adults have all worked out!).
- *Emotional control.* Teenagers will often act out a negative emotion instead of controlling the emotion. (This is closely related to impulse control.)

Temporal Lobe Development

Also underdeveloped in teenage brains are the temporal lobes, which are found behind the temples. The short story on the temporal lobes is that they're responsible for (among other things) emotional interpretation. This means teenagers have a physiological reason for not always understanding their own emotions and for being notoriously deficient at interpreting other peoples' emotions. (Guys, by the way, are significantly worse at this than girls are; in addition to the physiological reasons, it's cultural.)

Myelination and Neuron Winnowing

A third new finding is exceptionally fascinating to me. Neurons are the "wiring" of the brain. They're the microscopic conduits through which electrical pulses of information bits are transmitted throughout the brain. Bundles and pathways of neurons form into what are referred to as "neural pathways"—superhighways of thought, in a sense. During the young teen years, two remarkable things occur concerning neuron development.

The first is a process known as *myelination* or *myelinization.* Myelin is a "sheathing" that coats the outside of a neuron, which serves both to protect it, and—even more so—to accelerate its performance. This sheathing process occurs during the teenage years. Several years ago, my youth ministry colleagues and I met with an adolescent brain specialist over a period of several days. I asked that brain specialist to give me his guess at the percentage of increase in brain performance that occurs as a result of this process. He was reluctant to say. So I pushed him and asked, "Does it, like, *double* the speed at which information travels on neural pathways?" He responded, "Oh, no! It's more like a 200-times increase."

Then there's this crazy thing that happens with neuron development prior to and after puberty that's left my middle school ministry friends and me digging for implications. In the two years prior to puberty, the brain switches into a growth mode where it develops *millions* of additional neurons—way more than will be needed or even exist in the eventual adult brain. But at puberty the process reverses itself, and a multiyear winnowing process takes place.

One of the leading scientists on all this new brain stuff is a guy named Jay Giedd. He calls this winnowing a "use it or lose it" process.[10] In other words, the process by which the brain begins to reduce the number of neurons present (remember, neurons make up the pathways by which the brain processes information) is based on use. Those neurons and neural pathways that are well used in early adolescence remain. Those that are underused are eliminated.

This has *enormous* implications for us parents of young teens! Giedd (as well as the adolescent brain specialist with whom my middle school ministry peers and I met) confirms that, in a sense, by mid-adolescence a teenage brain is "hard-wired" for the way it will function throughout the rest of life. Many parents (and schools, and churches) have traditionally taken an approach to formation that emphasizes cramming kids full of as much "information" as possible, hoping it will "stick" and become a guiding force in their lives. But this "use it or lose it" principle tells us it's essential that the young teen years be about learning *how to think*. Thinking about process and asking questions of "What if?" and "Why?" are all critical. Discovery is the best learning mode (for emotional, relational, spiritual, or academic learning). If young teens exercise this part of their developing brains, then it will positively impact their lifelong thinking, their spiritual growth (remember, spiritual stuff is abstract), their emotional health, their relational maturity, and their desire to continue growing and learning.

So make room for "Why?" and "What if?" Those are questions of speculation (that brand-new but wimpy ability in young teens). Encourage discovery. Don't be threatened by questioned values and boundary-pushing. This is the best stuff of early-adolescent brain development.

Can you see why I'm so passionate about young teen ministry? I believe science has confirmed my calling (both as a youth worker and a parent) *and* my experience with real middle schoolers. High school is too late.[11] Middle school is make or break, baby.

At a junior high pastors' summit a few years ago, we asked that adolescent brain specialist how we could help teenagers develop their brain capacity. He listed three things: Make sure they get lots of sleep,[12] encourage good diet and exercise, and let them live with the consequences of their choices. Wow. There's a big chunk of our parenting strategy right there!

What This Doesn't Mean

As this brain research has reached a popular level, it's often been misunderstood and misapplied. An example of this was a full-page ad by a large automobile insurance company that ran in many newspapers a few years ago.[13] The ad showed a cute line drawing of a brain. There was one little puzzle-piece section missing, and it was shaped like a car. The copy at the top of the ad said: "Why do most 16-year-olds drive like they're *missing a part of their brain?* BECAUSE THEY ARE."

The copy went on to offer a cursory overview of frontal lobe underdevelopment in teenagers, and how they aren't capable of good judgment. Really, the whole thing was a poorly veiled attempt to justify higher insurance rates for teenage drivers; a way to placate the impact on parents' wallets with a come-alongside tone.

The ad was a cheap shot, in my opinion. And it typifies the wrong thinking that can come from these new discoveries.

Yes, there are physiological reasons for what we've always observed in teenagers—they struggle with judgment, they're impulsive, they have a hard time prioritizing, they aren't good at emotional interpretation or control. But these realities should not lead us to conclude that teenagers (and, for our purposes, young teens in particular) are *incapable* of these things. Our conclusion should be just the opposite.

Since we have scientific support for many adolescent behaviors, we should be patient and sympathetic. But we should also be *that much more committed* to helping our young teen children exercise these deficient, *but not absent,* life skills. Puh-leeze! This research gives us a reason to step it up, not get fatalistic. It's not that at some magical point in their mid-twenties, young adults suddenly have fully developed frontal and temporal lobes that allow them to make great choices, prioritize well, and become experts at emotional interpretation. The brain, including these underdeveloped parts, gains efficiency and ability through *use.*

Thinking about Maturity

The adolescent brain specialist I referred to earlier also gave my friends and me a helpful framework for thinking about maturity. He said, roughly:

- *Physical Maturity* comes to fruition between ages 16 and 18. This is when the body's full potential is in place. Practice can make it better, but the potential is there.
- *Knowledge Maturity* peaks at ages 18 to 20.
- But *Wisdom Maturity* peaks at age 25. Car rental companies won't rent a vehicle to anyone under 25 years old because they know this little fact.

A Small Wrench in the Works (Or, Chicken vs. Egg)

As if all these new scientific findings about the teenage brain weren't enough to take in, there's now significant controversy about the underlying assumptions of the findings. I'm bringing them in here not just because I think they're interesting (although they are); I'm bringing them in here because they have enormous parenting implications.

To simplify the controversy, it boils down to a chicken vs. egg question. Are teenage brains underdeveloped in these critical areas because that's how they've always been (we might say "God's design," or use the word *nature*)? Or, are teenage brains underdeveloped in these critical areas because we don't allow or expect youth to use those brain functions (what theorists would call *nurture*)? Most of the scientists who conducted and reported on brain scans—and most of the academic and popular reporting that flowed from these studies—*assumed* it was nature: This is how adolescent brains have always been; it's just that we're only now discovering it for the first time.

But other scientists have pushed back, declaring that the new findings *do not* give any evidence of the teenage brain always being this way.[14] They suggest (and I'm finding quite a bit of resonance with this idea—it's shaping my youth ministry thinking in substantive ways) that the weight of historical evidence would imply just the opposite, that we've made (by our culture, by our schooling approaches, by our parenting, by our media) teenage brains this way.

Robert Epstein, the leading voice of this tribe, goes on to lament the extension of adolescence in America, and to suggest that this trajectory is not helpful and is reversible (though it's very complex). I could write (and am thinking of writing) an entire book on this subject alone. But for our purposes in this book, I'm going to suggest we parents take this small bundle of approaches:

1. Learn more. Dig into more of the research on adolescent brain development, especially Barbara Strauch's *The Primal Teen* (Anchor, 2004) and Robert Epstein's *Teen 2.0* (Quill Driver Books, 2010). Wrestle with the implications and insights for your own parenting.
2. Parent within the cultural reality your child lives in. In other words, whether these underdeveloped teenage brain realities are nature or nurture, they still *are*. Be sensitive, understanding, and aware.
3. Be a countercultural parent. In other words, don't accept that postponed brain development is a given. Parent toward independence and adulthood by giving teens meaningful respon-

sibility and reasonable expectations, and by not removing the natural consequences (good or bad) of their choices.

A Wrap and a Toss

I hope you can see that I'm passionate about all this brain stuff—both the development of abstract thinking and the findings about adolescent brain development. I find that it affects *everything* I do in both middle school ministry in the church, and in my parenting: planning schedules, setting boundaries and even bedtimes, what I'll encourage and what I'll discourage, the language I use in both casual conversations and discipline, what I'll be transparent about and what I won't be transparent about, how I'll talk about spiritual stuff, and everything else. All this cognitive development stuff is *constantly* in the back of my mind in my own parenting and ministry, and I believe it's tremendously important for parents of young teens to be aware of these critical developmental issues.

And, as I wrote earlier, these changes in brain development lead directly to many of the other changes middle schoolers are trudging through, such as the emotional changes I'll address in the next chapter.

A FEW WORDS TO PARENTS

CAUGHT, NOT TAUGHT

Thinking back to middle school, I don't recall any "big talks" I had with my dad. But I do remember his gentle nature, and the way he would look me in the eyes when we talked. He always made an effort to get down on my level; and I remember that his talking to me that way made me feel less like a child and more like a man. I watched everything he did: The way he reacted when he stuck himself with a hook on our fishing trip, or his lack of a temper when he was cut off while driving in traffic. I don't recall a lot of the things he told me back then, but I do remember the values and character he modeled every day.

In youth ministry we sometimes call this the "caught, not taught" principle. Many of the lessons we teach on Sunday morning will be forgotten by the time Sunday lunch rolls around. However, the time spent with students, the relationship building and the things that they see in our everyday, normal life—that's the stuff we're really teaching them.

When it comes to spending time with your young teen, it's important to remember this principle. There are certain characteristics that we as parents want our children to embrace, including honor, truthfulness, kindness, patience, sensitivity (this list could go on and on). But the vast majority of the time these values must be caught, not taught. Certainly, talking about them isn't a bad thing! But, in order for them to really sink in and take root, they have to be modeled regularly by someone (usually an adult) in your young teen's life. As a parent, you have the greatest window of opportunity to be that influencer. God has placed you in a natural role of leadership and guidance in the life of your young teen.

There's a lot of talk these days about "quality time" and "being intentional" with your kids. The truth is, if you work to stay healthy in your relationship with God and you continually seek to model the characteristics of Christ in your own life, then every moment you spend with your young teen will be both intentional and quality time.

—Sean Meade is the president of Stuck in the Middle in Wichita, Kansas.

Chapter 5

Roller-Coaster Freak Show
(Emotional Development)

Not long ago, at my middle school guys' small group, a normally quiet and even-keeled Zack couldn't sit still. It wasn't merely a classic early adolescent case of the wiggles. He was downright plucky. He had a perma-grin on his face, and he kept drumming his fingers on anything and everything.

I knew he'd started attending a new school that day—an experience that would be challenging for most kids. So I asked him how it went. His response: "Well, I didn't get called a motherf---er even *one* time today!"

Same night, same small group: Bryson, a kid who has more energy and randomness than just about any other middle school boy I've ever met, told us—at a completely random point in our small group time—about the deep pain in his family because his dad had been partially paralyzed in a motorcycle accident several months earlier. Our group had been meeting for only about six weeks, and I didn't know Bryson's family. So this was brand-new information to me.

The funny thing about Bryson's tale was that he shared it in a lighthearted tone and with a chipper smile on his face. Of course, he's most likely got some deeper emotions he wasn't willing to reveal at that moment. But he didn't appear to be wearing a mask as he told us about his dad. It was just that his emotions didn't match his story; and he didn't have a clue about that reality.

Maybe you've observed, in your own young teen, one or more of these common for-instances:

The daughter who bursts into tears after you mention the pet cat you had as a child, because it reminds her of her neighbor's cat that died in a tragic road-crossing incident four years ago.

The son who broods in his self-selected isolation, but then suddenly comes alive and forgets his coolness while getting caught up with a puppy in the backyard of a relative's house.

The daughter who believes you're the coolest parent EV-AR and is happy to have you around, even with her friends; but who suddenly, and for no apparent reason, decides you're the biggest idiot to ever walk the planet.

The daughter who, on the first day of camp (as you hear later, from a camp counselor who's your friend), talks nonstop about being "in love with Tommy," then plunges into a broody depression on the second day of camp after a friend tells her she has been spurned, and then—later that evening—bounces back into "I'm a free agent" land now that it's clear "Tommy is such a loser."

The son who holds his emotional cards very close, like a sunglasses-wearing professional Texas Hold 'Em player, but innocently lets a little grin squeak out from time to time.

The daughter who goes through a phase where she offers frequent hugs and says, "Love ya!" to pretty much everything that moves.

These are all external signs of the massive internal shifts taking place in the minds and hearts of young teens. Their emotional landscape is undergoing a brutally thorough renovation, and it's confusing, messy, costly, intrusive, and harrowing.

Please know this: I didn't write the previous examples with disdain or condescension. And while the emotional roller coaster of early adolescence presents all kinds of interesting and unique challenges for those of us called to this ministry (and hear me, your parenting role *is* a ministry), I find it absolutely gorgeous and see the fingerprints of God all over it.

The Expanding Color Palette?

As a guy who likes visual images, I like to think the emotional shift taking place in the lives of middle schoolers is akin to a painter receiving a larger palette of colors.

Children and preteens, with their limited cognitive options (meaning, their more literal, concrete thinking), are like painters holding color palettes containing the primary colors and one or two others.[1] Sure, they can mix colors on the canvas, but those brush strokes are often unintentional at best.

Emotions are abstract. Or, more accurately: Thinking about emotions, or being self-aware of one's emotions, is even more abstract. A nine-year-old can certainly identify "I'm mad" and "I'm happy," but any more nuance than that gets a bit challenging. And when concrete thinkers *are* able to identify the sources of their emotions, they'll usually assume an external reason ("You made me mad" or "The puppy made me happy").

A couple of years ago, my family moved locally. We'd been in our house for almost seven years, so it was the only house my then-10-year-old son, Max, really knew. And it was a great house, with lots of room and an awesome pool. The day we finally moved, Max and I were the last two members of our family at the house. The new owner was poking around downstairs, and I was running around checking things out for a half-hour or so. When it was finally time to drive away for the last time, I realized I hadn't seen Max during that half-hour. I walked around looking for him.

I found him upstairs in his empty bedroom, lying spread-eagle in the middle of the floor, his eyes a little moist from emotion. I lay down next to him and asked him what he was doing. He was silent for a bit, and then he whispered, "I was just talking to my room, telling it how much I liked it."

Max and I talked about the strong emotion he was feeling over leaving our house. But he just didn't have the words to describe it. He's a very sensitive kid, and he feels strongly. But other than saying he was "sad" because we were leaving this house, he couldn't identify the details of what was going on in his heart—he only knew it was there and it was strong. It frustrated him that he didn't know how to explain it better.

With the cognitive development I wrote about in the last chapter, and the acquisition of a new, tiny, abstract-thinking "muscle," the options for *experiencing, understanding,* and *articulating* emotions expand dramatically.

Imagine that preteen painter with her little limited color palette. Then, without her actually realizing it, someone takes that old color palette away and replaces it with a significantly larger palette, one that's preloaded with a huge assortment of colors. New shades, new combinations, new possibilities.

And she starts painting.

But she has no prior experience applying these new color options to the canvas of life. So for a while, her painting is extra bold or extra muddled. She's creating art with patches of bright primary colors in one area of the canvas and subtle, nuanced shades in another. The combination is not always attractive, and sometimes it's even jarring. But this experimentation is necessary to get her to a place where she can effectively experience, understand, and articulate these new emotional possibilities.

Here's another metaphor.

I am *not* what anyone would consider a handyman. Other than replacing light bulbs and hanging pictures, I'm fairly useless when it comes to home maintenance or fixing things. And for years, the only tools I had were old hand-me-downs from my dad and grandpa: A few assorted screwdrivers, a couple of hammers, and a few other tools for which I could only guess a purpose.

A few years ago, my wife and kids bought me a new toolbox for Christmas. It's a cool plastic jobby with trays and little compartments that open to reveal neat little storage areas for various hardware bits. It came with a wad of new tools, and I subsequently procured more: Different kinds of wrenches and grips, drill bits and fasteners, strippers and pokey-things. I like my toolbox. I'm even proud of it—its presence on my workbench in the garage makes me feel a bit manlier.

But I still don't really know how to use much of the stuff in the box. I'm no more "handy" than I was before receiving my "now you're a real man" toolbox.

For young teens, it's as if they've just strapped on a massive tool belt, one that would make a contractor proud. They're walking around with all these new emotional tools at their fingertips. They like wearing the tool belt. They like having the tools on hand. They even pull them out from time to time and show them off or play "Bob the Builder" with them. But they don't really know what all the tools are or how to use them. They don't *understand* them. And because of that, they're likely to try hammering a nail into the wall with a wrench, or poking a new hole in a leather belt with a Phillips screwdriver.[2]

Emotional Whiplash

Of course you know what whiplash is—that painful neck condition brought on by a sudden and dramatic stopping or starting, usually in a car. And, of course, we use *whiplash* as a nontechnical, metaphorical word in lots of other ways (in discussing how we respond to any sudden, unexpected change).

With that framing, there's almost no better metaphor for young teen emotions than whiplash. It's not that every kid experiences every emotion suddenly and without warning. But this emotional whiplash is a common experience in the young teen years. And, unless they have an emotional disorder that brought on this kind of rapid emotional change during childhood, this dramatic encounter with their feelings is both new and not very welcome.

Just as with physical whiplash, emotional whiplash can leave middle schoolers with pain and a bit of disorientation. Because their abstract thinking is new and underdeveloped (and because, as I noted in the last chapter, their underdeveloped temporal lobes leave them a bit short on emotional interpretation), they have very limited knowledge of how to understand or control these feelings. It's very common for young teens to feel blindsided, or even betrayed, by their emotional experiences. We must understand this if we want to be effective in parenting our middle schoolers.

Parallel, in a sense, to the reality that their lack of cognitive ability shouldn't cause us to assume young teens are incapable of making good choices, prioritization, or speculation, we do them a disservice if we assume their whiplashy emotional experiences are just something to be tolerated in a fatalistic way. Instead, it becomes part of our mission to walk with them through these emotional blindsides, acting as emotional tour guides and emotional language tutors.

Fear of the Unknown?

As with so many of the other changes going on in the lives of middle schoolers, emotional change brings with it great opportunity and possibility, as well as fear. We all have a tendency toward fear when we're enmeshed in an experience of the unknown. Depending on individual personality, this can sometimes be a positive fear (such as the person who loves the fear associated with bungee jumping), or it can merely bring abject terror (a different person bungee jumping).

Most middle schoolers will tell you, in moments of honesty, that they don't understand why they're feeling such emotional intensity at times, or why particular emotions snuck up on them so fast or lingered so inexplicably long. They just don't have the experience or language to interpret this stuff.

Let me pause for a moment here, for a semi-related story about young teens trying to put words around their fears. My friend John was meeting with a group of student presenters who were all preparing for a large training event where they would be co-leading a room full of middle schoolers in understanding evangelism. At the upcoming event they would be asking all the middle schoolers in the room to identify any fears they had in relation to talking about faith with a friend. The student presenters were supposed to seed this discussion by sharing their own fears. So John asked his student presenters to talk about this in their prep time. Realize, these were eighth-grade student leaders—kids who were chosen for this role because of their maturity (in every way).

Two of John's student presenters "got it" immediately and shared things such as the fear of rejection or not knowing what to say. Then it was Doug's turn to share. He simply said, "Bees."

Surprised, John said, "What?"

Doug repeated his answer, "Bees. I'm afraid of bees."

John said, "Um, these are supposed to be fears about sharing our faith."

Doug said, "Yeah, I know; but I really am afraid of bees."

Classic.

Now, back to fear itself. Psychologists tell us the root of most fears is the unknown. When we don't know what will happen, or we can picture a negative outcome, we may experience fear. Therefore, we adults might experience fear when we wonder if ending a relationship might bring pain. We might experience fear when we stand at an ATM in the dark, wondering if we might get mugged. We may experience fear when we're unsure what the outcomes of a particular choice might be, especially if some of those outcomes are perceived as negative. But when we gain understanding of the unknown, or we move past the potential of negative outcomes, the fear dissipates.

Most adults don't tend to experience fear because of our emotions (unless perhaps we're afraid of what our emotions might lead us to do). But remember, young teens are seriously impeded in their ability to project outcomes. This can bring less fear at times (like the boy who doesn't think about how attempting to skateboard down a flight of stairs could easily result in a broken arm); but it can also bring a greatly heightened, although unarticulated, experience of fear.

Here's Normalization, Again

I realize I'm starting to sound like a broken record on this normalization thing. But the reality I've observed is that helping young teens normalize their experience is counterintuitive to most of us. It's our own "tiny muscle" that needs exercise and lots of use before it becomes part of our parenting norm. We have to choose, over and over again, to be conscious of normalizing before we'll be good at it in a more subconscious or unconscious way.

So how do we normalize emotional experience? I wrote a little about this in chapter 2, where I shared the story of my conversation with my daughter, Liesl, regarding her emotional outbursts. But let's review a bit here.

When it comes to young teen emotions, normalizing starts with acknowledging those emotions in healthy ways. The two unhealthy ends of the spectrum (which all parents of middle schoolers are well familiar with from their own challenging experiences with their kids) are—

- *Acknowledging emotions, but in a diminishing way.* Because we have more experience with emotions and understand them more fully, it's easy for us to see when a young teen's strong display of emotion (positive or negative) is way out of proportion to the particular experience generating it. And often our knee-jerk reaction is to tell kids they're overreacting, or they're being ridiculous, or they're being immature.[3] (Remember, maturity is behavior that's appropriate to development and age—so a young teen's emotional outbursts are actually mature.)
- *Ignoring emotions, especially extreme or unpleasant ones.* Since we know, or assume, the emotion isn't warranted—at least from our adult perspective—we're quick to dismiss or ignore it. While this approach isn't ultimately all that helpful, it's understandable, since we've seen how these extreme emotions often pass quickly.

Unfortunately, neither of these extremes is connected to a "come alongside" approach. If we envision our roles as emotional tour guides and emotional language tutors, then our response shifts to a more helpful place. But this requires us to live with a challenging engaged-but-disengaged tension. We want to be fully engaged with our middle schoolers in the midst of their emotions, even joining empathetically in their emotions. But at the same time, we need to remind ourselves, "This is not about me." Our kids' emotions can quickly affect *our own* emotions, which is fine and good when we're aware of it. But it's not helpful when we get swept up in our own emotional reactions. And that's true whether we are reacting against the emotions of our young teens, or when our own emotions parallel theirs.

The acknowledgment of emotions that we need starts with a calm response, something along the lines of "You're feeling pretty strongly about that, aren't you?" Often, it can be helpful to acknowledge through a question. "Hey, you seem pretty down. What are you feeling?" "What are you feeling that's making you so happy today?" Try to ask questions that get them to describe the feeling more, not just the external factors producing the feeling. (This is key, and it takes some practice.)

When young teens are willing to let you in a little (or a lot) on what they're feeling, it's great to make comments such as, "I've felt like that before," as long as that's a truthful statement.

Slip emotional acknowledgment into conversations by saying things such as, "That might cause you to totally freak out!" or "You've probably felt like this before." Pepper your conversations with this kind of generalized emotional acknowledgment.

And, of course, when appropriate, it's wonderful to *enter into* an emotion with a middle schooler. If she's mourning, even if it's a situation where her emotional response seems out of proportion to the incident, then mourn with her. If he's uncommonly happy and chatty, then match that emotion and go with the flow. This will be a very different experience than kids usually have, as they're more accustomed to adults responding to their emotions in one of those two extremes I wrote about a few paragraphs back.

Talk about this emotional development stuff head on. Make it a dinner or car conversation. Approach it the same way you might approach a conversation about physical change or sexual development—with sensitivity and frankness.

Actually, I like to take the normalization of emotions a step beyond, well, normal. I like to take it to "good." So often, normalization can come off as "grin and bear it" or as suggesting that some experience our kids are going through is just an unfortunate phase of life that they can only hope to emerge from. Instead, we parents want our normalization attempts to point kids to Jesus, to the Creator God who loves them so much that he wants them to experience life fully (John 10:10). We want our kids to see that this crazy emotional roller coaster they're experiencing is all part of God's loving plan to give them a rich and meaningful life that's full of great emotion. Really, how terrible would life be without emotion?

Control Versus Understanding

Just a short rant here.

I've often heard people say kids need to learn to "control their emotions." Of course, there's a sense in which this is true, and it will come, in time. But what I've observed is that the call for helping teenagers control their emotions very rarely comes from a place of caring about those teenagers. It's usually about the inconvenience of teenage emotions on the adults who are voicing this desire for "control." *And,* if I can push this a bit, it often comes from adults who have somewhat lost the ability to really be present in the midst of their own emotions. They equate their own ability to stuff emotions with controlling emotions, and they assume everyone else should do the same.

If we think back to Stephen Glenn's model of sampling, testing, and concluding (see chapter 2), we remember that the young teen years are all about sampling. Testing and concluding will come, eventually. No reason to rush into them.

So we should be more interested in helping our young teens *understand* their emotions than helping them control them. Remember, thinking about emotions is a new thing for them, and it's really hard work.

And in light of what we've learned about the "hard wiring" of the brain in regard to neuron winnowing (in chapter 4), I'd much rather see parents spend their energy helping their son or daughter develop the ability and practice of understanding, than the ability and practice of control.

In my opinion, control is overrated. And without understanding, control is wrongly fueled.

Rant over.

Differences between Guys and Girls

Gender differences play a role in most of the developmental areas I'm talking about (as was clear in the "Physical and Sexual Development" chapter). Sometimes the "mechanics" are the same for both genders in various realms of developmental change; but how they play out is often subtly or massively different for both physiological and cultural reasons.

I've seen some research that suggests that physiology plays a part in the differences we see in emotional development between guys and girls.[4] But there's still a lot of work to be done in this area. Certainly, we know that boys are 18 to 24 months behind girls in lots of developmental changes, including the brain functions that allow for, regulate, and interpret emotions.

But there also seem to be some strong cultural factors at play here. In Western cultures (especially in the United States), girls are taught from a young age to externalize their emotions, while boys are taught to internalize emotions. Group pressure, media, parental influence, sibling influence, and lots of other forces conspire (consciously or not) to tell guys it's not manly to cry or be emotionally expressive. It seems we tell our guys that anger is the only strong emotion that's acceptable to express. So boys quickly learn that they're expected to stuff their emotions, not express them.

There's lots of fear attached to this for middle school guys. Not wanting to run counter to any of these developmental norms, guys will find ways to mask their emotions even when they have strong feelings. In fact, some say "the guy code" is all about an "I'm fine" attitude.

Girls, on the other hand, are told to see their emotional expression as a means to an end. Externalized emotions are often "used" as a way of getting friends or keeping the ones they have. In a bit of a catch-22 risk, girls observe that strongly emotive girls are either wildly popular, or seen as freaks. It's a tough choice they have to make, and you can literally watch as middle school girls test their hypotheses about this. When girls shrink away from their emotions, it's often because they don't believe they have what it takes to use emotional expression as a means to a positive end. (In other words, it's often the result of a lower self-image or insecurity.) Girls who *do* express their emotions are often either confident in the result that this expression will bring, or they're merely rolling the dice that it will bring a desired result. (In some cases, especially among younger girls, they're merely clueless about how others perceive them.)

Do you see how this all connects with the abstract-thinking ability of perceiving how others see us? Middle schoolers aren't very good at this third-person perspective, so they (both boys and girls) often miscalculate the expected response from others. When adults experience others reacting to us differently than we'd hoped, we often change gears midstream and regulate our emotions. But kids are not only underdeveloped at "guessing" how their emotions will be received by others; they're also pretty weak at gauging real-time responses. So in the midst of a response that's different than what they expected or hoped for, they'll often "crank it up to 11" with the notion that more is better.

I'll talk more about this in the chapter on relational changes (chapter 6), but it's also important to realize that girls' friendships are formed with a high expectation of intimacy and self-revelation. Emotions, and emotional expression, are 100 percent essential to these expectations. As a result, expressing emotions in the context of friendships—or potential friendships—becomes a subconscious "tool" (I don't necessarily mean that in a negative way) that girls wield as relational glue. Boys, on the other hand, well...not so much.

Deeper Issues

I've written about all these emotional issues at a very popular level, as they pertain to an in-the-trenches parent with an average kid. But emotions are tricky things to generalize. As soon as we make one generalization or characterization, it's easy for you to find an exception.

Here's what you need to hear from me about exceptions: Not only are there exceptions, but good parents look for exceptions.

In the case of emotional development and expression, there are many possibilities for why a particular young teen's behavior might not match the general pattern. But it's important to realize that in general, a kid who shows outside-the-norm emotions—either too much or too little (a tricky thing to gauge, since they all seem to show "too much" or "too little" emotion at times)—may be tipping his hand that there are other serious issues that need to be addressed. The face-value issue we can see (what therapists call a "presenting issue") is often only an outer onion skin that covers deeper issues that have very little to do with the immediate situation.

Also, even "normal distribution kids" (when it comes to emotional expression) can have much deeper issues that need to be explored and may need to be dealt with by someone other than you. This is another reason why parents of young teens should engage with their children in the whats and whys of their emotions.

We can't make the potentially harmful assumption that a young teen's moodiness or low-grade depression or even super-happiness is merely the stuff of early adolescence. Emotions are clues to us, and they point us toward deeper conversations that may reveal abuse, clinical depression, or difficult life circumstances.

It's sometimes wise for parents to have a professional "go to"—a therapist or psychologist with whom they can have a chat about their child. Most of us (myself included) aren't trained to deal with serious issues. We can't assume our empathy and compassion alone will be enough for young teens with serious emotional issues. Ask for advice and know when to seek help.

A FEW WORDS TO PARENTS

THAT'S WHAT MY MOM SAID!

It's the end of a youth group event. As everyone is leaving, a young teen hangs back to talk to her youth worker about an issue she's having at school. After the youth worker listens to the story and offers her counsel, the middle schooler says, "That's what my mom said!"

I have had countless conversations like this with kids in my youth group. During these conversations I often wish I had a video camera, or a hidden microphone, so I could show the evidence to the student's parent. It would be documented proof that this middle schooler is actually listening to her parents.

Middle schoolers are entering a time in their lives where they're becoming more self-aware. They see themselves as individuals, and search out ways to declare their independence. Middle schoolers' first steps toward exercising this independence may include picking out their own clothes, deciding what music they listen to, and choosing which friends they want to hang out with. As they experience this new time of making their own decisions, they begin to wrestle with their need for parental advice and how to get it while maintaining their path toward independence.

Yes, young teens do have a wider group of people they can turn to for advice, such as friends, teachers, and youth workers; but the value of the counsel they get is given weight by the relationship with the one giving it. That's why the advice they lean on the most is—whether it feels this way to you or not—from their parents. This is the counsel they carry with them and use as a backstop for every other piece of advice that comes their way.

In terms of feedback, your young teen may give you no more than a grunt or an eye-roll, or may even just leave the room without a word. But I know your son or daughter is listening, and it's making a difference in his or her life. Someday, that young teen may use a piece of advice she learned from you and actually change the world. At least that's what *my* mom always said.

*—Christina Robertson is the middle school pastor
at Journey Community Church in La Mesa, California.*

Chapter 6

Best Friends Forever!
(Relational Change)

Tom and Joanne, two caring and engaged parents, sat in my office. With them was Christopher, their seventh-grade son. "Topher," as he'd recently asked his friends to call him, was slouching in his chair, arms crossed, with a look on his face that radiated "I'd rather be *anywhere* other than here" behind a thinly veiled attempt at looking bored.

Joanne started talking. "I'm very concerned about our Christopher."

"Topher," Christopher mumbled.

Joanne ignored this and continued, "We're not even sure who he *is* anymore. It seems like just yesterday he was this sweet kid who wanted to be around us and loved family time. He was helpful around the house. And he was consistently happy."

Topher rolled his eyes.

"But he's so withdrawn now. And the thing that really scares us is that he seems so committed to swapping out all his good friends for new ones—and these new 'friends' aren't the kind of kids we want him hanging around. They're not a good influence on Christopher." (She actually made air quotes with her fingers on the word *friends*.)

"Who says they're not a good influence, Mom?" Topher shot back. "You don't know them. You just want me to hang around that loser, Sean!"

"Honey," Joanne turned to her son, "Sean is not a loser. He's been your best friend since kindergarten. You've played together for *years*. And he still wants to be your friend. But you're *so mean* to him now. It just breaks my heart."

"Mom, Sean was fine as a friend when we were little kids. But *everyone* knows he's a loser now. And if I hang around with him, everyone will think I'm a loser, too!"

Obviously, there were lots of issues swirling around in this little exchange. Christopher was wrestling with new emotions he didn't have words for; he was struggling to gain some new independence from his parents, and they were struggling with how much independence to give him. (More on that in the next chapter.) But Christopher was also articulating the relational shift that occurs in the lives of young teens.

Like the other shifts happening in their lives, this relational shift is often fraught with confusion and fear, with desperation and failure, with experimentation and discovery.

Christopher was explaining, in the words of a young teen, that the reasons one chooses a friend in childhood don't often hold up in the world of early adolescence.

Proximity Versus Affinity

Like so many other changes going on in the lives of middle schoolers, these relational changes are directly tied to cognitive development. As their brains begin giving them peeks into abstract thinking, young teens begin exercising a different set of criteria for friendship selection, a set of criteria that's much more adult in nature.

To oversimplify: Childhood friendships are normally formed around proximity. Children choose friendships based on those they're near most often. Of course, this is a generalization, and other factors play in. But because children are less differentiated and don't possess an external perception of themselves (at least not an articulated third-person perception), they're often fine forming friendships with a neighbor or someone they spend a lot of time with (like the child of a family friend), even though they may have extremely differing personalities and interests as they grow up.

Put five seven-year-olds in a room with a pile of Legos, and they'll usually find a way to play together just fine. Their interests are less diversified. And each one's sense of self is rather unarticulated.

But put those same five kids in a room together five years later, as 12-year-olds, and the situation is very different. They "dance" around one another, trying to find alliances and political influences. It's suddenly a game of *Survivor* with all the drama and second-guessing and questions of "Who can I trust?"

Instead of proximity, middle schoolers begin to form friendships based on affinity.[1] They want to form friendships with those who share their interests. Of course, this is a big challenge, since young teens rarely have a clear sense of their own identity and what their interests actually are—they just have a sense of what they'd like their interests to be.

Christopher, in the example at the beginning of this chapter, was talking, quite clearly, about this shift. He might be fine hanging out with Sean if he were certain no one would ever know. But his perception that others consider Sean a loser carries such enormous weight in Christopher's own attempt to define himself that he can't risk being defined by his affiliation with Sean. Sean would drag him down and relegate him to loser status.

This shift often brings a literal change in friendships during the young teen years. Formerly meaningful childhood friendships are often jettisoned, as young teens reach out for new, and often tenuous, attempts at friendship. Of course, there are kids who maintain childhood friendships throughout their teen years; but it's very normal for those childhood relationships to simply be unsustainable in adolescence.

Multiple Affinity Groups

While young teens are wrestling with what it means to form friendships around affinity, they often dabble in multiple affinities. This is all part of that discovery mode I've mentioned several times. They're very unclear about who they are, and, as a result, they find it very challenging to align with any particular affinity group.

When my daughter, Liesl, was a young teen, she seemed to have three different personalities. When she was with her school friends, she adopted a particular set of values, language, preferences, and behaviors. When she was with her small group from our church, she adapted and embodied a slightly different set of values, language, preferences, and behaviors. And when she was with just our family, there was a third set of values, language, preferences, and behaviors. Now, as a 16-year-old in eleventh grade, Liesl's three sets of "norms" are already substantially less differentiated from each other than when she was 12, as she's becoming more comfortable with who she is.

It's the wrong question to ask which of these was "the real Liesl." Were she an adult, we'd be correct in assuming that one is real and the others are not (or that they're all a mask and the *real* Liesl is something still other). But this isn't the case with young teens. Each of those three manifestations was Liesl. She was trying them all on, like different wardrobes, in an attempt to discover more about herself.

It's very normal to find young teens playing with multiple affinities and switching styles and personalities along the way. One week a boy will clearly want to be perceived as a skateboard dude, with the accompanying clothing, music preferences, language, and attitudes. A month later, this seems to have been shelved and an attempt is being made to be über soccer guy. Or the proto-emo. Or sensitive artsy guy. Or chick magnet. Or wannabe gangsta dude. Keeping up with these shifts can be exhausting.

And when, from our adult perspective, we see the short-lived, not-fully-embraced nature of these passing affinities, it's easy to dismiss them. But a dismissive attitude isn't any more helpful than assuming that any of these outward manifestations is the whole story and the real kid. We need to affirm their quests, while also looking through and beyond the externals to the real kid behind the often temporary multiple affinities.

The Role of Self-Perception

I've hinted at this already, but it bears fleshing out a bit more: A big reason for these relational changes is the new influence of self-perception.

As I wrote in earlier chapters, it would be wrong to say that identity begins forming in early adolescence. Identity is being formed from Day One of life, and childhood relationships, roles, expectations, observations, and media intake all play a gargantuan role in forming aspects of one's identity. But the shift that occurs with the onset of abstract thinking is enormous: It's the first time in life that we have the ability to think about our own identity formation. It's the first time we can really say, "This is the kind of person I want to be, and these choices will move me in that direction."

In other words, puberty brings with it the abstract-thinking skill of self-perception. A preteen's ideas about how others perceive her are based only on observation (how others treat her, what others say about her). But an abstract thinker can now perceive herself from another person's perspective.

I want to be clear about this because it's an important difference. Nine-year-old Tammy might have a sense of what her friend Jenna thinks about her. But this perception is solely based on external indicators, such as—

- Jenna's desire to spend time with Tammy, both face-to-face and in the virtual world;
- Jenna's willingness to share secrets with Tammy; and
- Jenna's comments that Tammy is fun, pretty, and more adventurous than Jenna is.

Now compare that to Tammy's experience when she is 14. She now has the ability to exercise an empathetic perspective. She can place herself in Jenna's shoes, so to speak, and think about what life is like for Jenna (whom Tammy perceives to be a great friend, but a bit quiet and reserved). And Tammy can ruminate on thoughts, such as—

- Since Jenna is quiet, she probably wishes she were more outgoing like I am.
- Since Jenna is less adventurous than I am, I'm the leader in our friendship.
- Jenna really likes to IM and text a lot. This is probably because I'm one of her only friends. I can choose to abuse that or

manipulate her, or I can honor that special place and protect Jenna.

Tammy might not be quite as mentally articulate as I've described here; however, loosely formed third-person thoughts about herself, from her friend's perspective, become a shaping force in Tammy's identity formation and self-image.

And, to take it one step further, young teens start to subconsciously understand that they can influence others' perceptions of them and—in essence—change or direct who they are. In fact, this growing realization can either be energizing or shattering. Tammy might find great confidence in realizing she has a real responsibility in how Jenna perceives her. Or this new awareness can bring a sense of helplessness if she begins to believe she should be able to influence others' perceptions of her but can't influence those perceptions in the direction she desires.

Remember, this abstract-thinking ability is new, and it's weak. Kids jump in and out of abstract thinking for years. So the reality is that Tammy will continue to rely heavily on her nine-year-old indicators while she's starting to develop some of these self-perception abilities.

And in many ways, this is a lifelong struggle for most of us. We vacillate between a self-perception based on external input from others, and a self-perception based on what we know about ourselves or who we desire to become.

Of course, as our young teens develop these new self-perception framing abilities, it's super-important that we parents talk about identity issues with them. Keep your conversations with your child about who she is and who she's becoming anchored in God's design in creating her (rather than humanity's sinful impulses after the fall). Remind him of who God made him to be and that his identity should ultimately be informed and formed in the context of God's perfect love for him. Help her see herself as part of a community that needs her. Remind him that God didn't mess up when God made him.

Girls' Friendships

Fairly significant gender differences seem to emerge in early adolescence concerning how friendships are formed. Some of this is physiological, and rooted in gender differences regarding how women and men connect with others; but lots of it is rooted in cultural expectations for how girls and guys are supposed to act.[2]

For instance, young teen girl friendships are deeply connected to girls' desire for intimacy. As a result, girls' friendships require a high level of intimacy, commitment, perceived trust, and transparency. Middle school girls often form friendships based on shared intimate or transparent shared experiences. This is definitely not the case with guys (more on that in a minute).

So middle school girls tend to form intense, highly vulnerable and intimate friendships, bonding deeply and strongly and quickly. And, I've observed, middle school girls tend to have these intimate friendships with one or two other girls (forming a friendship group of two or three girls). Girls love having BFFs—"best friends forever!"

But a friendship group of four or more middle school girls usually can't sustain its own emotional weight. Gossip and insecurity are enormous factors. And since they're in a discovery phase of life, young teen girls are playing with their identities, which means these intense friendships are often short-lived and transitory. A friendship group of four middle school girls will usually split into two groups of two or a group of three (where the fourth girl moves on to another friendship group or is forced out).

So it would be fair to say that middle school girls form small, intense friendship groups with high expectations of exclusivity, intimacy, and commitment; but these friendships are often temporary. This isn't true with all girls, of course. Some form friendship bonds with one or two other girls that last throughout early adolescence (and, occasionally, into the older teen years). But for most young teen girls, some ebb and flow in this transitory landscape of friendships is normal.

It's important for us parents (and especially for moms) to help young teen girls understand the value of friendships that aren't temporary or dependent on developmental changes. But of course this means helping them understand the skills required to stick with a friendship through the challenges inherent in all friendships: Disagreements and fights, perceived or real betrayal, changing interests, and the place of other friends (who are usually perceived as competition).

Friendship structures are just one of the many areas that are changing in the world of middle school girls today. That's why I've asked Kara Powell and Brad Griffin to write a "guest chapter" addressing new issues facing young teen girls. You'll find that "bonus chapter" at the end of the book, beginning on page 175.

Guys' Friendships

The friendships of middle school guys tend to be very different from those of their female counterparts. Again, part of this is physiological. As previously noted, guys tend to be a good 18 to 24 months behind girls in pubertal development. This means abstract thinking develops later in guys, so their self-perception and ability to speculate on third-person perception is also lagging behind the girls'.

But the larger reason guys form friendships differently is connected to our cultural expectations about what it means to be a guy. Guys learn to internalize their emotions (whereas girls often wear their emotions on their sleeves) and put on the mask of "the guy code" that says, "It's cool; I'm fine."[3] Most guys grow up in a substantially more isolated world than girls do. And this is particularly true in the United States, where we have a marked low-trust culture and place high value on individual rights and personal autonomy.[4]

I've observed that middle school guys tend to fall into one of two extremes when it comes to friendships. The first is what I like to call "the wolf pack." This is a large-ish affinity group of guys—four to eight in size, usually—that forms around external affinities, rather than personal sharing and intimacy. And along with that organizing force there may come a whole raft of language, clothing, values, music, behaviors, attitudes, interaction styles, and boundaries.

We're the guys who are into skateboarding.

We're the guys who are bored and brooding.

We're the guys who are consumed by gaming.

We're the guys who are into soccer above all other things.

We're the guys who are proto-emos.

We're the guys who like to light things on fire.

These affinity groups—wolf packs—often define everything for boys. Remember, as I mentioned earlier in this chapter, they may not stay in the same affinity group for their entire early adolescent experience. And they're sometimes dabbling in multiple groups at the same time (although, usually only one group in any particular setting, such as school, church, or sports).

There's a synergy that happens in these groups, and they're often collectively single-minded, destroying everything in their path as they amoeba toward a goal of conformity.

The other extreme I see in so many middle school guys is the loner. This is the young teen guy who really doesn't have any significant friendships. He may have a guy or two whom he considers a friend, a guy he occasionally games with, or a guy he went paintballing with once (and both of them now perceive that they go paintballing with each other "all the time"). But he lives in a relationally isolated world, masking his feelings and hiding his interests in the fear of being shunned. And my observation is that this "classification" is increasing: More and more middle school guys have no real friendships.

I'm convinced that good parents of middle school boys need to be intentional about helping their sons form meaningful friendships. We need to talk about the attitudes and skills of a friend. And since guys usually form friendships by doing things together (rather than by sharing things about themselves), we need to provide opportunities for shared experiences that foster friendships. We need to encourage potential friendships, fertilizing the relational and emotional ground that's often left untended.

My own middle school son falls into this category, and it causes him more emotional stress than anything else in his life. He desperately wants to have friends, but finds the constantly shifting terrain of middle school social life to be fraught with unpredictability and disappointment. So my wife and I go out of our way—including driving many more miles in our car than we would prefer—to provide opportunities for Max to hang with other boys. (For us, this is exacerbated by the fact that Max attends a private school, where his potential friends live in a 45-minute radius from our home.) And we talk about it with Max regularly, giving him a safe space to express his sadness or excitement, never trivializing his experience with a condescending "you'll be fine" comment.

Here's a startling fact: The average teenage girl uses approximately 20,000 words a day. Girls connect by talking, form relationships through verbal interaction, and process their feelings by talking about them. On the other hand, the average adolescent guy uses approximately 4,000 words a day.[5]

Simply put: Girls form friendships by talking; guys form friendships by doing. While we shouldn't play into these norms blindly, and we should still provide opportunities for guys to use words and learn to express themselves, we also need to be aware of the natural inclinations that exist in their worlds.

A FEW WORDS TO PARENTS

PARENTING AT REST

When people hear that I work with middle schoolers, they often say to me, "God bless you. I could never do that." My response is usually, "Working with young teens is fun—parenting is the *really* hard work." And now that I have a preteen in my own home, I know I'm about to step onto a whole new playing field!

I believe one of the biggest mistakes parents of young teens can make is thinking our primary responsibility is to control the behavior of our kids. We tend to feel a great deal of pressure to keep our kids from moving outside God's moral boundaries and to tell them what kind of people they need to be. But by focusing on controlling the outward behavior of our young teens, we create a great deal of stress and often hinder their development.

In their book *Making Peace with Your Teenager,* Kevin Huggins and Phil Landrum wrote, "The most important task facing our kids during adolescence is to decide what kind of people they are going to be for the rest of their lives." We want to support our kids in growing into the kind of people God wants them to be, but in the meantime, we're often tempted to try to take every important decision away from our kids, to decide for them. This can easily create power struggles that, in the end, cause us to lose control and influence over our middle schooler, rather than gaining it. And when we parent this way, our young teens never have the opportunity to learn to take true responsibility for their own decisions.

God calls us to a different approach to parenting our young teens: a position of rest that allows us to loosen the reins and trust that God is working in the lives of our kids. Such an approach recognizes that, although we parents care deeply about the kind of people our young teens decide to be, we can't control how they make their decisions. And the good news is this: We don't need to be in control; because in the end, God is in control. Parenting at rest frees us to be an ally to our kids, to give them resources, guidance, and support that will help them grow into the kind of people God has created them to be.

If we parent from pressure, if we think *we* need to get it right all the time, we minimize the work of the Holy Spirit in the daily lives of our kids. However, when we parent from a position of rest, we trust that God is working in the life of our child from the inside out, which will eventually bring about maturity.

When we are truly at rest, and parent from this position of trust, all the pressure that we sometimes put on our kids and ourselves will be placed on God. This approach is not done in a lazy or apathetic manner. This is about shifting the responsibility back to God where it ultimately belongs. With each problem we face with our middle schooler, we have to continually shift from self-reliance, to reliance on God. And modeling for our children what it means to rely on God is one of the most important things we can do as parents.

—Alan Ramsey is the pastor of students and middle school at Fellowship Church in Knoxville, Tennessee.

Chapter 7

I Can Do It! Just Don't Leave Me
(Independence)

Long ago, I discovered that middle schoolers believe hotels are extremely cool. It doesn't have to be a fancy hotel—any roadside roach bomb will do. And many of the more family-friendly national chains have a "kids under 18 stay free!" policy (which certainly wasn't created with youth workers in mind, but, ya know, it's a nice loophole).

For many years I utilized the occasional hotel for a middle school ministry trip or event. (For instance, when en route to a mission trip or staying in town with a group of boys for an all-night video game fest.) When I did, I created a couple of guidelines for myself and other adults volunteering in the ministry: Adult leaders couldn't share a bed with a kid (either the leader could sleep on the floor or the kids could), and we always had one leader for every two rooms of kids (with an open adjoining door between the rooms).

But then we had an out-of-town event with too many kids for the number of leaders. There was no way to enforce my "one leader for every two rooms" rule (which usually amounted to about a 1:7 ratio). So my team and I came up with a new security measure that allowed middle schoolers to stay unchaperoned in a hotel room. The security measure: Cellophane tape.

The kids were stoked about staying in this hotel and having a bit of freedom and independence. When it came time to herd them into their rooms for the night, we explained the limits of their freedom: They were in charge of themselves for the night, but we'd be accessible if they needed us. They could choose their own bedtime and decide when to get up. (We'd give all the rooms a wake-up call at some point.) They could order pizza if they wanted, but it had to be delivered to their room by midnight.

Because…

We told them we were going to place a small piece of cellophane tape between their room door and the doorframe at midnight. This little piece of tape—we assured them—would not "seal them in." If there were an emergency, the doors would open as easily as if the tape weren't there. But when the adults made a few rounds during the night and a final check at 6 a.m., we'd know if they'd opened the door for any reason at all. And the occupants of any room where the tape wasn't in place would have to sit out for two hours at the beginning of the next day—at a water park.

Of course, the response was as if we'd said we were going to shackle each of them with leather straps and straitjackets. They cried out about how *unfair* this was, about how we didn't trust them.

Our response: "We *do* trust you, within the boundaries of your hotel room. And we want to remove the temptation to try something stupid outside of your rooms, which would create problems for all of us."[1]

The first time we tried this experiment, a few kids "checked" to see if the tape was there. This was a hard lesson, as they quickly learned there was no way to reapply the tape from the inside. In subsequent years, we never had any doors opened, and the groaning morphed into a happy acceptance of this boundary. With big smiles they'd ask, "Are you going to tape us into our rooms again?"

This example is both a literal illustration and a metaphor. It's a literal illustration of how I chose to give kids both freedom and boundaries in a youth ministry context. But it's also a metaphor of the tension that exists between the independence young teens *want* and the boundaries they *need*.

The Point of Adolescence

In a simple sense, adolescence is the culturally approved pause button between the reasonably carefree life of a child and the responsibilities of adulthood. I wrote about this at more length in my book for youth workers called *Youth Ministry 3.0* (Zondervan, 2008). But for our purposes here, let's look at it this way:

Carefree life of a child = Dependence

Responsibilities of adulthood = Independence

Adolescence is the space between those two states, and it lasts for however long culture (and parents) approves. To that end—while it's a little simplistic—the transition from dependence to independence is the whole point of adolescence. In fact, the adolescent experience has become our culturally approved rite of passage. And since it's a transitional period, it should include a mixture of both dependence and independence.

If we were to imagine adolescence as a line graph, with puberty on one end and emerging adulthood on the other, we would see a progression from dependence to independence along the way. In other words, the young teen years have—and should have—more dependence (and less independence) than the older teen years.

Whatever the ideal mixture (more on this in a bit), the reality is that young teens want more independence. This, once again, is directly tied to their cognitive abilities, as well as cultural factors.

First, their expanding sense of self (as described in the last chapter) provides the opportunity to see a direct connection between their choices and their identity—who they are and who they're becoming. They begin to see how they play a role in shaping themselves, that they have a choice in who they are and who they're perceived to be.

Second, they start to wrestle with a distinctly adolescent task: Autonomy.[2] The task of autonomy is about asking—and answering—these questions:

- How am I unique from others?
- What's the extent of my power to influence myself, others, and my world?

Struggling with these questions requires some amount of abstract thinking. There's really no way to think about one's uniqueness or the extent of one's power without some ability to exercise third-person perception. Psychologists talk about *individuation*.[3] This is a ten-dollar word for the process of becoming one's own self, and it includes self-knowledge and a somewhat functional understanding of autonomy.

I've heard it said that the goal of parenting teenagers is to help them become independent. While I'm sure there are other supplemental goals, this does seem to make some sense.

I remember talking to a dad I deeply respected. I'd been so impressed with his kids, who were in high school at the time. I knew his daughter best, who was then about 16 or 17 years old. So I was surprised when her dad said, "Really, my job is pretty much done. Of course I need to stay involved and continue to love her; but my years of influence, if I've done my job well as a parent, are mostly over."

This was reorienting for me in many ways. Not being a parent of a teenager myself at the time, I'd perceived parents exerting a large influence on their kids throughout adolescence. But if I'm right about that changing mixture of dependence and independence (with puberty on one end and emerging adulthood on the other), then the latter end would be mostly independent.

Of course, this also means the end of that continuum nearer to childhood should have large portions of dependence, even if young teens don't appear to want it.

What Do They Really Want?

Young teens *need* boundaries, but they want freedom—and there's a massive tension here. (Just imagine Mel Gibson's character from *Braveheart* shouting, "FREEDOM!") But the reality is, young teens believe they want more freedom than is actually healthy for them.

Young teens with too much freedom (read: too much independence) often flounder because they don't yet have the ability or perspective to make good choices with unlimited options. Remember, their abstract-thinking ability is very new and wimpy. And their frontal lobes—the decision center of the brain (see the end of chapter

4)—are still very underdeveloped. When we give them more limited options, we greatly increase their ability to exercise wisdom.

Think of it this way: If you put a puppy in an enclosed yard, it can experience a sense of freedom. There's plenty of room to explore, plenty of opportunity to go this way or that way, to run or walk or lie down, to bark or be silent. But place that same puppy in the middle of a massive open park, and the puppy will lack any kind of reference points for choosing where to go. It might end up running in circles and chasing its own tail; or it very well might run off and get completely lost, having no sense of the ramifications of running nonstop in any particular direction.

It's only with *well-defined* boundaries that middle schoolers are able to effectively exercise some sense of independence. A lack of boundaries creates confusion, fear, and danger.

Young teens *want* boundaries. This might seem counterintuitive. And you'd be hard-pressed to find a young teen who could articulate, "Please, give me more well-defined boundaries." But, ultimately, middle schoolers are more content and confident when they understand the extent of their control. And because they haven't worked out that autonomy task yet, their understanding of their ability to control is greatly limited and notoriously unreliable.

The goal is to slowly increase those well-defined boundaries. As a middle schooler gets comfortable with some freedom, she's ready to have the boundaries widened. This process should be repeated, gradually and continually, throughout adolescence.

"From everyone who has been given much, much will be demanded; and from the one who has been entrusted with much, much more will be asked" (Luke 12:48) seems an appropriate bit of Jesus wisdom here. If we parents give too much independence, too quickly, then our middle schoolers will crumble under the requirements.

Independence Isn't a Challenge for Kids Alone

Here's a no-duh reminder that still might be helpful: Independence isn't just something to be exercised; it's something to be given or granted. In other words, for middle schoolers to move out of dependence, someone has to give them independence. It's a transaction, in a sense.

We, as parents of young teens, are the primary "givers" of independence. And let's be clear here: This is one of the most difficult aspects of parenting a teenager. Even the best parents struggle with where to set the boundaries. Thoughtful, engaged parents err in both directions, and they often feel a bit helpless in knowing how much independence to grant. I've heard countless parents express this to me over the years. And now that I have teenagers myself, I live it every day.

As a youth worker who understands the importance of coming alongside parents, I regularly have to remind myself not to assume parents are intentionally drawing boundaries that are too tight or too loose when it comes to independence. Most of us parents are just trying to figure it out, and we can use all the support and grace we can find.

I do, however, often run into two extremes in parenting styles that are equally harmful to the healthy development of young teens.

Harmful Extreme 1: Smother

The first extreme is the parent who draws the boundaries too small, not offering the opportunity for any real independence or decision making. In most cases, these parents have good intentions.[4] Their desire is to allow their children to hold on to their innocence and remain children as long as possible, rather than rushing them into adolescence. These "smothering" parents are usually well aware of the cultural pressure on young teens to act like older teenagers and to participate in and be exposed to behaviors and options that aren't age-appropriate. This is a good inclination, when it's set in the proper context and perspective.

My wife and I made the difficult choice to move our daughter from the public middle school she'd been attending to a more sheltered private school about six weeks prior to the end of her sixth-grade year. We made this choice, in part, because our daughter is a natural risk-taker (one of her strengths), and she was quickly drawn to all the behaviors, values, and attitudes of older kids as soon as she was exposed to them. In other words, her "boundaries" were massively expanding, beyond what she was ready for, and she was naturally inclined to rush all the way to the fence (and hang over it a bit).

We feel we made this choice just in time, as Liesl was able to rebound and rediscover some of her age-appropriate innocence. It was as if she'd started to play at older teenage behavior, values, and attitudes, but she hadn't fully taken them on yet. When we moved her into a more protected environment, she flourished with the more age-appropriate amount of freedom she was granted.

Of course, the extreme is not healthy or helpful. The extreme is the parent who doesn't allow her child any real freedoms and keeps her child's choices limited to those appropriate for a fifth-grader. If that's you, even if your motivations are good, you're damaging the growth of your child.

Harmful Extreme 2: Total Freedom

The other extreme is just as harmful, or maybe even more so. And, certainly, I'm seeing this extreme played out with greater frequency than ever before. This is the parent who says, "I don't know how much freedom to give. My son wants total freedom. And it sure seems as though his friends have that. So I guess, since he's a teenager now, total freedom is what I should give him."

Oof. The result is the lost puppy in the park.

As with the smothering approach, the motives are often good: Parents want to encourage their young teens to exercise independence. They may be operating out of fear of losing a connection with their kids, or out of exasperation over constant fighting, or out of ignorance or disinterest. But whatever the case, I am regularly shocked by the number of 12- and 13-year-olds who seem to have almost complete freedom in decision making. Sure, they still rely on their parents for food, shelter, and rides to the mall. But they have no boundaries when it comes to time use, media consumption, food intake, texting and phone use, bedtime, room décor, friendship choices, and a host of other should-be-boundaried choice realms.

Young teens with total freedom are often stunted in developing good decision-making skills. Because the playing field is so open and wide, they find it difficult to connect consequences with their choices. So, in a sense, this boundary-less freedom actually impedes the healthiest course of growing in wisdom.

Of course, this doesn't even cover the multitude of truly bad decisions young teens could make with total freedom, which could have significant long-term consequences. Then again, my observation is that parents who err in this direction also tend to make the mistake of removing the natural consequences of their children's bad choices, thereby doubling the error. (More about that later.)

A Couple of Suggestions

This independence thing is a big deal—and it's the source of sleepless nights and deep frustration for many parents. So let me say just a bit more before we move on.

First, you may have noticed that this chapter talks less about culture and other factors than other chapters. That's because this particular issue is so strikingly connected to parenting. The parent factor in regard to this developmental shift is 100 percent inexorably integral. It's impossible to consider the quest for independence apart from the dynamic give-and-take being played out between middle schoolers and their parents or guardians.

With that in mind, let me make two suggestions:

1. Adopt a curious perspective when considering your own motives. What's really behind, or underneath, your approach to boundary setting? What issues from your own teenage years are playing in? Are you reacting against what you didn't like? And—this is a tough one—do you really want to see your son or daughter move toward independence, or would you rather (if you're fully honest) have them continue to depend on you, as that can provide perceived value and identity stability? If you're married, talk with your spouse about your motives.

2. Engage in conversation with other parents about these tricky boundary questions. If you're part of a church with a youth ministry, ask if they would host a parent dialogue, and have

a couple of youth group leaders sit in to give input from their own perspective. Or, have dinner with another couple or two, who, from your observation, seem to have done a good job with this journey. Ask them grace-filled questions about their attempts to walk this fine line. Talk with them about the concept of freedom within well-defined boundaries, and about how those boundaries need to expand over time. Ask them to describe times when they placed the boundaries too tight, or times when they hadn't clearly defined boundaries (even the best parents err in both directions from time to time).

The Challenge of Choices

Young teens need opportunities to make choices if they're ever going to learn to make *good* choices. This means, of course, that they're going to make some *bad* choices. So it's critical that we create an environment in our homes and the lives of our middle schoolers where a few things are present.

Give Them Choices

It's great parenting to give kids the chance to make choices. This might include choices regarding their clothing, hairstyle, hobbies, use of their personal funds, priorities in free-time use, scheduling chores—even input on family decisions like vacations or major purchases. Remember, we're tour guides to the young teen experience. That means we offer our middle schoolers choices and then walk alongside them, giving input when sought and encouragement always.

Allow Them to Fail

Failure is a major part of learning. In fact, my contention is that most of us learn much more from failure than we do from success.

A few years ago, I was part of a discussion with a group of seasoned youth workers who were developing the content for a day-long youth ministry training event that would be attended by 20,000 youth workers in cities across North America. The theme was what real transformation looks like in teens, so we started by talking about significant times of spiritual transformation in our own lives. When the list was compiled, we realized that deep transformation seems to take place, most often, in four contexts:

- Community
- Perspective-altering experiences
- Victory and success
- Failure and pain

As parents, we should be actively pursuing opportunities to engage with our young teens in all four of these arenas, or at least shepherding them into contexts where they'll experience those things. But, wait—should we shepherd them into contexts where they'll experience failure and pain? Well, not directly. ("Here, Johnny, I know you'll fail at this, but it will be good for you!") But, knowing that failure and pain are prime teachers, we parents *must* be intentional about being ready to engage with our middle schoolers when they experience failure and pain (and, of course, they will). What would it look like for your home to be a place where it is *safe* to fail and to talk about failure?

Allow for Natural Consequences

We need to be intentional about allowing our middle schoolers to experience the natural consequences of their choices—while we walk alongside them as they do so. Remember that adolescent brain doctor I wrote about in chapter 4? He said one of the *only* things we can do to help the development of the decision-making center of the brain is allow kids to experience the consequences of their choices. Our natural inclination as parents—because we love our children and because walking with them through their consequences is much harder—is to remove the consequences. But we do them and their development a disservice when we do this.

A quick first-person adolescent story before we move on.

When I was 16 and got my driver's license, I convinced my dad to let me take the family Volkswagen Bug on a driving date. This was two weeks after I got my license. I picked up my date at her house, and then I drove a half-hour to a large new shopping mall where we had dinner and went to a movie. When the movie got out, the mall was closed. So we walked to the car in the back of the now-empty parking lot.

The mall had a huge parking lot surrounding it and a circle drive around the outside, like the glaze on a donut. I was driving around the perimeter, heading for the exit, when I remembered a math lesson: The shortest distance between two points is a straight line. But I was driving an arc. So I turned into the empty lot, cutting across rows of empty parking spots, and made a 50-mile-an-hour beeline for the exit.

Except, I didn't see the traffic island. I thought it was just a line painted on the ground. Just before I hit it, I realized it was actually a cement curb about 18 inches high and 10 feet across.

As I slammed the Bug into the parking island, I ripped all four wheels, both axles, and part of the drive train off the car. The underside of the car skidded along the pavement before coming to a skewed stop.[5]

Long story, short: My dad was going to sell the car the next week. So he made me buy it from him for his full asking price. I made monthly payments to him throughout the following year. I was not happy about this. But in hindsight, I'm glad he didn't remove the difficult consequence of my actions because I've never driven fast through an empty parking lot again. As an adult, I've even thanked him for his courage, which was borne out calmly and with love, not in anger.

School Shift Comes Around: K–8 to JH to MS to K–8

Schools are wrestling with the best approach to this independence issue, too. And there are varied opinions about what's best for middle-school-aged kids.

Historically, kids in what we now consider the young teen years were in primary schools (now called elementary schools). There was no real separation of children until secondary school (now called high school).

As high schools became mandatory and the number of students increased, "junior" high schools popped up, providing an intermediate space between elementary and high school, where age-appropriate learning, as well as freedoms, could be experienced. The middle school movement of the 1980s (and beyond) began to lobby for a schooling approach that was less about preparation for high school, and more about developmentally appropriate education and the "right" mix of dependence and independence (as well as the inclusion of sixth grade, in response to the average age drop in puberty). And this continues to be the dominant approach to education in both public and private schools.[6]

However, a new/old approach is getting a lot of buzz these days. It's the old K–8 approach, which keeps "middle schoolers" in a school with their elementary counterparts, while allowing them some additional freedoms and responsibilities. This seems to be a mostly good attempt to allow them to be young longer, not rushing the preteens and young teens into adolescence in a way that junior high schools or middle schools seem to do. There's a bit of a *Lord of the Flies* vibe that takes place in a normal middle school; and the K–8 approach is an attempt to postpone that.

This shift usually means fewer freedoms for middle school kids in these K–8 schools; but conversely, it also brings more responsibility, as they're often called upon to play a mentoring role with the younger students. I'm intrigued by this direction (my daughter attended a K–8 school after we moved her at the end of sixth grade, and my son currently does). It will be interesting to see how this evolves as the larger culture continues to shift in its understanding of preteens and young teens.

A Fly in the Ointment: Independence and Community

One final bit here in this chapter—just a question to mess you up a bit.

Should independence really be our goal?

To state it another way: Is independence a *biblical* value or an American value? Certainly, it's an American value. But I believe you'd be hard-pressed to make a strong case for it being a biblical value. Community, yes. But independence? Not so much.

So what do we do with this? Certainly, learning to take responsibility for oneself is at the core of the adolescent experience, at least in our culture. (And remember, there was no "adolescence" in the time when the Bible was written.)

I don't have a great answer to this question. I believe it's a tension we have to live with. We need to help our kids develop independence, while remaining suspicious of our culture's obsession with independence. We are people of community, and our identity is one of being *the people of God,* not individual, disconnected, Lone Ranger-like sons and daughters of God.

Hmmm. Let's all think about that one a bit more.

GIVE 'EM SOME SLACK!

A few years ago I took up indoor rock climbing as a hobby. This type of climbing is never done alone; so the first thing I learned was how to belay. The "belay" is the person on the ground who holds the safety of the climber in his hands. As the climber scales the wall, the belay passes the rope to the climber to allow for some slack, or places tension on the rope to keep the climber from a devastating fall.

Belaying is a great picture of our role in balancing your young teen's desired autonomy and her necessary dependence. You, as a parent, are a belay. The trick is to know how much slack or tension to provide, and when. Sometimes parents make the mistake of holding their kids too tight, restricting their freedom to move and, ultimately, hindering their development. As parents we need to look for times and places where we can give slack to our young teens to let them try new things on their own that will help them move toward independence.

It's okay—and even necessary—to let your middle schooler attempt new things and sometimes even fail. In the right situations, failure can be a great tool for learning. But we still have to be there to add tension when needed, helping our young teens make decisions that are developmentally over their heads and avoid dangerous situations that could be harmful. Giving your young teen the right amount of slack matched with the correct tension will help you as you parent your child toward independence.

—Mark Janzen is the student ministries team leader
at Willingdon Church in Willingdon, British Columbia.

Chapter 8
Operating System Upgrade
(Spiritual Development)

When I was in ninth grade, I went on a two-week wilderness trip in the Appalachian Mountains. We carried everything in backpacks and spent the time hiking, canoeing, climbing, and learning about ourselves.

One day, after a long and arduous uphill hike through thick forest cover, we emerged just before sunset at a high promontory with a massive panoramic view of a valley bathed in early evening light. It was breathtaking; and we all stopped and stood in silence, just taking in the view, the fresh air, the warm feeling of accomplishment, and a shared experience.

There was lots of work to be done for the evening (camp to set up, meal to cook, plans to talk about for the next day). Still, the evening would have been just about perfect, except for one thing: We were hopelessly lost. We were without our adult leader on this day, and we'd gotten ourselves completely disoriented.

Yet even amid all this confusion and uncertainty and added responsibilities, it was still a moment dripping with possibility, with greatness, with a new awareness of expansiveness.

This works as a metaphor for what's going on in the spiritual development of young teens. And, as is true with most of these developmental issues, the revolution of middle schoolers' faith is directly tied to their cognitive development.

Abstract Faith

Stop to think about it: What, if any, aspects of faith *aren't* abstract? Sure, children can have a very real and concrete faith. And that's good and age appropriate. But you wouldn't want to have a child's understanding of spiritual things. There's a difference between the childlike faith that Jesus praises (Matthew 18:1-4) and childish faith.

Choose a faith topic, anything from discipleship to the incarnation, from salvation to the Trinity: *They're all abstract.* You can (and should) use all kinds of concrete images when describing something like the Trinity to young teens: "It's like an egg. There's a shell, white, and yolk; but it's still one egg," or, "It's like water, steam, and ice—three forms of one substance." But these cute little efforts at concretizing the abstract concept of the Trinity still leave us substantially short of actually understanding the interdependence and relationality of a three-in-one God.

This challenge doesn't matter so much for preteens and children. They're fine with a simplistic, concrete understanding of faith things. They're fine with seeing a black-and-white version of an issue that's deeply and richly nuanced with color because the black-and-white version is all they're capable of grasping. It works for preteens. But the new ability of abstract thinking that comes with the onset of puberty changes everything. It takes young teens to a surprising vista (not all at once—usually in bits and pieces) where everything gets reframed.

In a positive sense, this shift is exciting (both for them and for us), as it opens up new opportunities for understanding, ownership, application, and implication. Viewed from a more challenging perspective, this spiritual shift is disconcerting and confusing because it necessarily calls into question childhood beliefs that no longer work or no longer make sense. And remember, young teens have the ability to think abstractly, but it's a wimpy, underused ability. They don't toggle switch into full-on abstract thought one night while they're sleeping. So they tentatively step in and out of abstract thought on a regular basis, advancing and retreating.

You'll notice flashes of abstract faith understanding in your young teen (as was the case with Garrett in chapter 4). And if you check for understanding when talking about abstract spiritual stuff with your son or daughter, you'll often find that they're squishing your abstract discussion to fit their thoroughly concrete childhood thinking models.

A New Operating System

The best way I've found to think about this shift is to compare it to a change in the operating system of a computer. The operating system runs in the background and informs all the programs you use and see on your computer. You don't *see* the operating system, per se, but it shapes your use of all the other programs.

I am typing on a MacBook Pro right now. I "went Mac" a few years ago, after well more than a decade of PC use. And just recently, I got an operating system upgrade to Apple's newest OS, commonly called "Snow Leopard." (This will quickly date this book.)

But I still have plenty of old documents (PowerPoint presentations, word processing docs, spreadsheets, and so on) saved on my laptop's hard drive from years past. Some of them are in a PC format, and some are in an older Mac format. When I open one of these older documents, my computer takes an extra second to convert the file into a format my current operating system can utilize. Then, if I make any changes, a window pops up and asks me if I want to save the file in the old format or the new format.

In fact, one more element exists now that I'm using "Snow Leopard": The new documents I create aren't readable in the old operating system. If I saved this manuscript in the new format and sent it to someone who uses an older format, that person wouldn't be able to open it. I need to go through the additional step of *choosing* to save the document in a format that can be read by both the older and newer operating systems.

This is *a perfect metaphor for* what's going on in the spiritual development of middle schoolers.

The Challenge to Johnny's Systematic Theology

Let's put this into a case study of a middle school kid.

All preteens, no matter what faith system they do or don't subscribe to, are in a time of concluding. And as such, preteens have a somewhat concluded, worked-out worldview. You might even call it a systematic theology. A preteen has great confidence in his understanding (as wrong or simplistic as it might be) about how the world works, relational dynamics, power, and spiritual stuff. Ask a Christian preteen to explain the Trinity, and she'll have no problem. She'll even think you're a little weird or dumb for believing there's any reason *not* to understand this concept. Easy peasy lemon squeezy. All i's dotted and t's crossed.

So meet Johnny. Great kid. Johnny has had a robust faith as a preteen, one that's beautiful and age appropriate and wonderfully childlike. Johnny is traveling through life with his little backpack of faith. And in that backpack, Johnny has stuffed his cobbled-together systematic theology, his fairly definitive understanding of all things spiritual. And it works for him.

One thing Johnny has come to believe is that prayer works. (This is a great thing!) Johnny believes God answers his prayers. Johnny also believes that if he asks God for something—and it's not selfish—then God will give it to him. (Johnny knows this doesn't mean he can just ask for a new skateboard, duh!)

But in the fall of Johnny's seventh-grade year, his favorite grandpa is diagnosed with advanced inoperable cancer and given a couple of months to live. Although he's a bit disoriented by this initially (because Johnny also has a simple belief that good things happen to good people, and he knows his grandpa is really, really good), Johnny grows confident that if he asks God to heal his grandpa, God will do so.

Johnny prays and prays and prays. But his grandpa still dies. Suddenly, that faith bit is pulled out of Johnny's backpack of faith and examined.[1] Johnny considers the clash between his previous belief about how prayer works and the reality he's just experienced. He now has three options:

1. Johnny can conclude, *Well, my understanding of prayer didn't quite work. But it's all I have, so it will have to do.* Then Johnny stuffs his simplistic faith bit about prayer back into his backpack of faith. Years of repeating this choice is what leads kids

to the unarticulated, mushy faith that Christian Smith calls "Moralistic Therapeutic Deism."[2] Such unexamined faith is often carried into adulthood—which is why most churches are full of adults who attend worship services and subscribe to a basic set of moral guiding principles but lack an articulated, active faith that affects their daily lives.

2. Johnny's second option is to conclude, *Well, this doesn't make sense anymore. But I don't have anything to replace it with, so I'll just chuck it.* This is why we have so many older teenagers and young adults who leave the church or jettison their faith. By the time they actually walk away from the Christian faith, they've typically gone through years of discarding this belief system—bit by bit. Their childish faith just isn't sustainable in the real world of a 19-year-old. And, really, why should it be?

3. Johnny's third option is the most difficult—and this is why spiritual engagement with your middle schooler is so important. Johnny can go through the challenging process of evaluating his faith bit by bit and working to find a new, more adult-like (abstract) way to frame his understanding of prayer. This work of faith evolution, of growing in understanding and articulation, is a bumpy, potholed road with plenty of opportunities for misunderstanding and frustration. And it's a process for which Johnny *absolutely needs* adult "coaches"—whether they're his parents, his youth leaders, or other adults—who walk alongside him and help him sort this stuff out.

The Role of Speculation in Faith Formation

There's a cycle we all go through when we're learning something new, and it pertains to spiritual matters as well. We consider a truth or an idea or the implications of an experience, and eventually it shows up in our lives as a new understanding, a new perspective, a new behavior, a new value—or, in the case of spiritual stuff, a deeper faith. This "cycle of learning" has specific implications for middle schoolers, as there are a few steps in the process that are natural for adults but don't come easily for young teens.

Here's the cycle:[3]

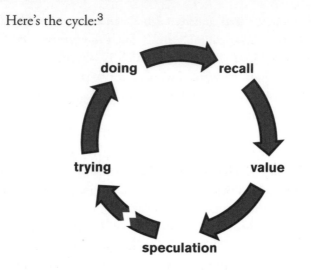

Recall

The process of learning starts with recall (in other words, some bit of data). It could be a biblical truth in the context of teaching or a conversation. It could be an experience. It could be a narrative of some sort. But some piece of data provides an entry point for potential learning (and, in our context here, for spiritual growth).

Unfortunately, many parents (and teachers, and youth workers) wrongly make the assumption (or at least work from the assumption) that it's normal for us to go from information to a changed life. While I agree with Scripture that God's Word will not return void (Isaiah 55:11 NKJV), and that the Holy Spirit can do whatever the Holy Spirit chooses to do, there are normally additional steps in the process through which truth (in the form of the Bible, experience, narrative, nature, and other truth exposures) shows up as change in our lives, minds, and hearts.

Value

The second step of the learning process is one we don't often think about when it comes to middle schoolers, yet it's extra important. The "value" step (which psychologists call "affect") is one of emotionally connecting or "adding value" to the data.

At this very moment, you're crossing this hurdle as you read this book. You're adding value to the learning process of this book because you care about the subject material, and you care about your middle schooler. You're naturally incented to care about this subject, based on your interests and values as a parent of a young teen.

We'd like to believe young teens will attach value to the learning process (or any spiritual growth opportunity) because they value the subject matter itself. But no matter how stunning your family devotional on the book of Numbers may be, the reality is that most middle schoolers are *not* going to attach value to a learning experience based simply on the subject matter itself.[4] This is a little less true with data that comes from experience, rather than a teaching topic. But the valuing step is still a big hurdle.

Lucky for us, this valuing can occur another way: It can come from the learner (in this case, your middle schooler) attaching value to the learning *process,* rather than the subject itself. *And* this "valuing the learning process" can happen simply because your son or daughter values his or her relationship with you.

For example, your daughter might be sitting in the backseat of your car on the way to the mall as you talk about something you read in the Bible this morning. She might care very little about the actual content of the biblical truth. But let's assume you're an engaged parent, and your relationship with your daughter is meaningful to her. She knows (at least at a subconscious level) that you care about this biblical truth, that you believe it's important. As a result, your daughter can attach value to the learning process simply because she knows *you* value it. (Do you need any better rationale for a parenting approach rooted in relational engagement?)

Speculation

The third step in the learning cycle is speculation. (Now we're gettin' to the good stuff of middle school faith development!) Speculation is simply asking the "what if" questions. It's the conscious or subconscious process of considering the data (again, a truth or experience or other input) and what implications it could have for her life.

Here are a couple of simple examples:

Josh is in a small group, and they're talking about what it means to be a good friend. Speculation is Josh merely thinking about the questions: "What does it look like for a middle schooler to be a good friend?" or, more specifically, "What would it look like for me to be a good friend?"

Emily is standing at the head of the line at the soup kitchen where her youth group is serving breakfast. She's handing out trays to the homeless people as they enter the serving area. A homeless woman smiles at Emily and says, "Thank you, sweetie. You're an angel." Emily starts to think about what it would mean to change her ideas about homeless people.

Hey, if you haven't read the chapter on cognitive development (chapter 4), then you really need to go back and read that now. It's impossible for us to talk about speculation and middle schoolers without framing it in the realities of how new and challenging the abstract-thinking process of speculation is for young teens.

Here's the harsh reality: The speculation step of the learning process (or the spiritual growth process—there really isn't a difference for our purposes here) can't be skipped; but young teens stink at speculation. Here's the "duh" point: We have to be extra intentional about what I like to call "taking them to the shores of speculation." We parents have to help our middle schoolers exercise their speculation muscles.

Young teens are capable of speculation, but they rarely go there on their own. So constantly working guided speculation into conversations is a huge part of effective middle school parenting. This means frequently asking, "Why do you think that?" and, "What would that look like?" and other questions that will tee up speculation.

The Knowing–Doing Gap

After the speculation step, you'll notice a little break in the next arrow. That break represents the gap between knowledge and action—or the "knowing–doing gap." Everything up to this point is cognitive activity. But on the other side, we try on new behaviors (much like trying on a shirt in a store to see if it fits you both in size and style). And beyond "trying" we move to "doing," where the behavior or understanding or value or perspective is now a part of who we are.[5]

This "knowing–doing gap" is a big challenge in middle school faith development. Speculating about what a new behavior (value, understanding, or perspective) might be and then *actually trying it on* won't come naturally to them.

Do you see how your growing knowledge of early adolescent development affects every aspect of your parenting of young teens? Whew!

The Importance and Beauty of Doubt

Tom and Barb, the parents of an eighth-grade guy named Stephen, sat with me at a coffee shop. They'd asked to meet with me to get some input on "what was happening to their son" (Barb's words) and to "join forces on a solution" (Tom's words).

Stephen had been a fairly regular part of our middle school ministry for three years, and he'd grown up in our church. He wasn't exactly a student leader or a kid who exhibited a passionate and articulated faith. But he wasn't a big problem in our ministry either. Until recently, he seemed to be nominally interested, at best, and blissfully ignorant of the fact that he was coasting into adolescence with a loose grasp on an inherited faith (the faith he'd picked up in his home, rather than one he owned himself).

But in the last couple of months, I'd seen a change in Stephen, and so had his small group leader. He was asking more questions about faith stuff. And because he was a middle schooler, Stephen was often asking these questions (or offering comments that revealed a hidden question) in ways that were passive-aggressive or combative. Stephen's small group would be talking about some Jesus-y subject, and Stephen would pop off with a comment like, "I don't even know why we'd bother." When I was teaching up front, there'd been a few times when I'd noticed Stephen rolling his eyes dramatically or crossing his arms in defiance. I'd had one quick conversation with Stephen about what was going on, and he'd said something like, "I don't know...I just have all this stuff I've heard my whole life, and I'm starting to have a hard time believing it's true."

Back to the coffee shop. Tom started: "Stephen has always been a good Christian boy. He's been willing to participate in our family devotions and to pray out loud at dinner. But he's shown a real change in the last few months, and we're greatly concerned."

Then Barb burst into tears. Her eyes had welled up the moment Tom began talking; but now they flooded out, and she momentarily held her face in her hands. When she caught her breath, Barb continued in Tom's place: "Stephen loved Jesus. I know he did! But do you know what he said the other night? Tom asked him to pray at the dinner table, and Stephen answered, 'I'm not sure I want to be a Christian anymore, so I'm not sure I should pray.'"

I'll admit now that what I said next was not the shining moment of my middle school ministry years. I don't believe I was being very sensitive to the fear and concern that were very real to Tom and Barb.

I smiled (that stopped them) and calmly said, "That's fantastic."

There was a long awkward silence as Tom and Barb tried to sort this out, wondering whether I was the Devil incarnate—or, at the very least, the newfound cause of their son's waning faith.

I continued, "Sorry, that was a bit abrupt. And I know this is very difficult and painful for you as parents because you love Stephen and genuinely want him to experience life in Christ."

Then I went on to talk about the absolutely critical nature of questions and doubt in the formation of early adolescents. Not that every middle schooler has to consider completely chucking her faith. But the journey from inherited faith to owned faith always goes through a process of questioning and often goes through a series of doubts.

In the church (and in many of our homes) we have a tendency to make kids (or anyone else) feel guilty for expressing doubts, as if doubt is sinful. Not only is this theologically wrong, but it's harmful to the spiritual development of young teens. If we shun them or guilt them for expressing a doubt or question, they quickly learn—

- *It's not safe to talk about questions or doubts. Even if I have them, I should keep them to myself.*
- *It's wrong to have questions or doubts, and my only two choices are to "be a good Christian" (which must mean ignoring or stuffing my questions and doubts) or reject the whole thing.*

Obviously, we don't want those results. So we need to be willing to walk alongside our kids as they express their doubts. And rather than thinking of doubts as a problem to be avoided, we need to view them as a *good* and *helpful* part of faith development—especially when young teens are willing to talk about them and give us the opportunity to process with them.

Of course, young teens don't always express their questions and doubts in healthy ways because they don't have the emotional maturity or clarity of thought to do so. So their articulation of questions and doubts often comes out in ways that can push our buttons and make us feel insecure. It takes maturity on our part to realize that our kids' button-pushing statements usually have nothing to do with us, even if they seem to be directed at us. We have to learn to look past the "presenting evidence" and be attentive to the very real questions and doubts that drive those comments.

This, of course, is easier said than done.

Thomas Wanted Proof

I like to consider how Jesus handled Thomas's doubt. You remember the scenario: Jesus had risen from the dead, and the Marys and a bunch of the disciples had seen him. But Thomas wasn't there when Jesus appeared to the other disciples. And when the others reported how they'd seen and talked with Jesus, Tom said, basically, "I don't believe it; and I *won't* believe it until I have physical evidence. I'll believe it when I can put my fingers in the nail holes in his hands, and my hand in the sword hole in his side."[6]

Then Jesus shows up again. Can you imagine what Thomas was feeling and thinking at that moment? Whatever doubts he had would have instantly vanished. I picture it going down like this:

Jesus: Thomas, I want you to come touch these nail holes and
this sword wound.

Thomas: Uh, Jesus, that's not necessary now. I can see you.
I'm sorry I doubted; but I, uh, was kind of exaggerating
when I said those things. You know, it was kind of like
that language you use sometimes, like when you said
we should pluck out our eye if it causes us to sin?

Jesus (still serious, but with a twinkle in his eyes): Thomas,
I'm serious—come over here now.

(Thomas shuffles forward. He's uncomfortable that everyone
is watching him and a bit grossed out by the impending reality of sticking his fingers and hands in those wounds. Jesus
gently but firmly takes Thomas's hand and guides it to the
wounds.)

Thomas (urgently): My Lord! I believe!

Jesus (with a smile and a little wink): Okay, we're done with
that now, Thomas. You can put that doubt behind you.

This is a great example for us. We acknowledge the questions and
doubts young teens have as real. We don't downplay them, dismiss
them, ridicule them, or heap guilt on them. We use them as opportunities for interaction. We walk alongside young teens, guiding them
as they process their doubts and questions. Then, once the doubt
is resolved, a new understanding is reached, or there's a realization
that sometimes doubt is something we just get to live with (none of
which tend to occur in one sitting, by the way), we help our kids have
confidence in what they've discovered.

Three Generalized Paths

As with Johnny and his three different ways of understanding
answered prayer (played out earlier in this chapter), I believe there
are three paths middle schoolers can take in their faith development.
I don't have numerous statistical studies to back up this contention,
although it seems to resonate with Christian Smith's work (referenced previously). And one might say it's based on the observational

research I've conducted with thousands of young teens and middle teens over many years of ministry.

I'm convinced kids who have grown up with some kind of Christian faith have to question and reevaluate that faith and come to some sense of a revised, owned, semi-articulated faith by the time they're 15 or 16 years old. Otherwise, they'll likely move toward one of the two other options Johnny had—cling to a childish faith or just chuck faith altogether.

If middle schoolers (and this also includes slightly older teens) don't rearticulate their faith, then it's quite possible that they'll move into a simplistic kind of moralization that's more about karma than it is about living in the way of Jesus. Or they'll simply jettison their faith as irrelevant, a holdover from childhood that—like dolls, Transformers, and security blankets—no longer makes sense to their almost-emerging adult world.

On the one hand, this is the weightiness of our calling as parents. This is the crux of the importance of parenting a middle schooler. But at the same time, we can take comfort in knowing that we aren't the Savior (nor are we the Holy Spirit). Our role is *not* to make kids change or force them (as in, manipulate them) to change. Honestly, we're not capable of that; and any perceived "results" of such strong-arm tactics will be shallow and short-lived.

Instead, we walk with humility and compassion alongside our sons and daughters as they trudge through this messy, disorienting, and beautiful transition in faith development. And as we do, we must be aware that what we think we see is often not the whole story.

A FEW WORDS TO PARENTS

SPIRITUAL CONVERSATIONS

If you're like most parents, you would like to have good conversations with your kids. The challenge is figuring out how to help those conversations happen. And the challenge looms even larger when it comes to talking about faith.

Unfortunately, when it comes to family discussions about faith, mum is often the word. The relatively small number of parents who *do* talk with their kids about faith tend to default to asking their kids questions:

What did you talk about in church today?
How was youth group?
What did you think of the sermon?

Depending on the personality and mood of your middle schooler, responses usually range from grunts to "the usual." Not very satisfying for you or your kid.

At the Fuller Youth Institute, our Sticky Faith research shows that asking these questions can pay off. But even more vital to your kids' developing faith is that you as a parent also share about your own faith. In other words, don't just interview your kids; discuss your own faith journey, too—including all its ups and downs.

Typically when I talk about the fruit that comes from sharing about your own faith, parents will chime in that they believe *living out* their faith in front of their kids is more important than merely talking about it. I would agree. I am 100 percent convinced that, as a parent, who you are is far more important than what you say. If I had to choose between either living out my faith in front of my kids or talking about my faith with them, I'd choose the former every time. But I don't have to choose. And neither do you. We can do both.

Recently I met a couple that has decided to be as transparent as possible in talking with their kids about their lives and faith journeys. The mom, Kathy, was raised in a family that talked about everything when she was young—everything, that is, except sex. As Kathy grew older, she ended up feeling like she couldn't talk about a lot of other things with her mom. It was almost like the degree to which her mom felt comfortable talking about sex was the degree to which Kathy felt comfortable talking to her mom about other things. In some sort of conversational swimming pool, the depth Kathy's mom would take in a conversation about sex set the maximum depth for their overall relationship. Kathy and her husband are committed to a different approach, one where they're willing to talk about the awkward stuff, knowing that the deep end of the conversational pool will result in a stronger and more open relationship with their teenagers.

Even though I sometimes mess up, I want to go as deep as possible in conversation with my kids—no matter what the topic is. Don't you?

—Kara Powell is a veteran middle school youth worker, and the executive director of the Fuller Youth Institute, in Pasadena, California. Kara adapted this sidebar from her book STICKY FAITH (Zondervan, 2011).

Chapter 9

White-Hot Temporary
(Early Adolescent Culture)

Whenever I talk to parents about the early adolescent experience, I seem to find one of two extreme responses in their thinking. Either they believe *nothing* has changed, and today's young teens are basically the same and dealing with the same things they were dealing with in their 11-to-14 years. Or they believe *everything* has changed, and nothing is the same at all.

As you might expect, I believe both are true. Or, more accurately, since those two extremes don't allow for each other, I believe both are true in the sense that there is much about the early adolescent experience and young teen culture that has remained constant across the generations, even while there is also much about the experience and culture of today's young teens that's markedly different than even 10 years ago.

What's the Same?

A few stories...

When I was in eighth grade, my friends pushed me into asking a girl named Sue to "go with me." (That's what we called steady girlfriend-boyfriend relationships.) I'd liked many girls, and a couple of them even liked me back. But I'd never taken this step, one that I perceived to be *huge* and *life changing*.

One day Sue and I were together as our youth group went on a daylong outing—horseback riding. I remember being crazy nervous as she and I walked around the corral and I tried to get up the nerve and find the words. If my memory serves me, I'm pretty sure I finally said something like, "Well, everyone thinks we should go together." (Romantic, huh?) Then, as my heartbeat rose to dangerous levels, I continued, "So, what do you think?"

My memory definitely serves me when it comes to Sue's response. She shrugged her shoulders and said, "Okay, I guess so."

And that was it! We were official. It lasted about a week.

Later that year, I acted on a crush I had on a girl named Kathy who was way out of my league (at least in my perception). She was popular, and she was…a cheerleader. She'd been "going with" a guy named Doug for a *long time* (which, in middle school, was probably about six months). But they'd broken up, and she was on the rebound.

Through friends, we'd made our interest in each other known. I knew it was the expected time for me to act. So one night while I was baby-sitting, after the kids were in bed, I called Kathy on the phone. We made small talk for a while, and I tried to get up the courage to ask her to "go with me." Finally, in a burst of now-or-never courage, I got out the words, "I have something to ask you."

She said, "Okay."

And I froze. I mean, I completely choked! My mouth was open, but the words simply wouldn't come out. So I did what came naturally: I hung up.

I quickly dug around in the cabinets of the house where I was baby-sitting and found a tape recorder. (Remember those little cassette recorders with the clunky buttons on the front? This was before boom boxes, by the way.) I used the tape recorder to practice asking Kathy out. I tried it a dozen ways, playing the recording back and listening for the right vibe and words. When I was convinced I had it nailed and I'd be the most suave and manly asker in the history of the world, I called her back.

I made up some reason for hanging up earlier (a kid was crying, or something like that, since this was prior to cell phones and the always plausible excuse that the call got dropped). Then I restated my intention, "I have something to ask you."

Again, Kathy responded with, "Okay."

And I froze again! I was trying to form the words and sound like that cool stud muffin from the recording, but it wasn't happening. Instead, I uttered a few "acks" and other noises.

Kathy said, "Are you still there?"

Finally, in a moment of panic, I grabbed the tape recorder, held it up to the phone, and pushed play. Unfortunately, I hadn't set the volume for this scenario, and my tinny recorded voice came booming out at a ridiculous volume: "KATHY, I REALLY LIKE YOU…" At this point, I scrambled and started adjusting the little volume thumbwheel, which provided a wonderful scratchy sound as the volume plummeted to a whisper, right through my perfect sentence, "Will you go with me?"

Despite all that, she said yes, and we "went together" for two weeks. Then she broke up with me and got back together with Doug. (I toilet-papered Doug's house throughout high school.)

One more story, just so these aren't all about my awkwardness around girls!

In seventh grade my buddies and I went on a guys' weekend outing with our youth group. We stayed at a rustic camp an hour away from our church. I don't remember much about the trip—other than that I sledded straight into a tree and almost knocked myself unconscious. But I do remember what we did to my best friend, John, utilizing our brilliant (not!) speculation abilities, well-articulated judgment (not!), and massive need for discovery and experimentation (yes!).

One night—who knows where our counselor was—we grabbed John, who was substantially smaller than the rest of us, and shoved him deep into his sleeping bag. Whenever we tried to pull pranks on John, he had a way of not caring. This usually diffused the situation or infuriated us. But in this case, it worked to our favor. We picked him up, still encased in his sleeping bag, and hauled him outside like three little Santas carrying a large sack of gifts.

The camp had a large flagpole near the dining hall. It stood about two stories high, and it had a little cement pad at the bottom. Since it was nighttime, the pole was barren. So we carried the bag-o-John to the flagpole, untied the ropes from their lashing points, and wound them around the end of the sleeping bag. The one thing we did right that night was to tie great knots!

Then, with John now coming to life and starting to get nervous, the three of us pulled the rope, heaving and grunting and laughing as we raised John—inside the sleeping bag—to the top of the pole. He later told us he was very confused as he realized our voices were getting farther away, and he could tell he was hanging from something.

I *think* our plan was to tie off the rope and stand there laughing for a while, amazed at our own brilliance and unquestionable hilarity. But once we got John to the tippy-top of the pole, we'd expended all possible gripping and holding power. Someone said, "I can't hold on any longer!" and we all looked at each other in panic, just as all three of us let go of the rope simultaneously.

We clearly weren't thinking things through; but at least we had the wherewithal to step back so John's plummeting body bag wouldn't land on us.

The good ending of what could have been the most horrible story of my young teen years: John broke his arm, nothing more.

Here's my point in telling these true stories from my own young teen years. I can totally see the middle schoolers I work with today living these exact same stories (except the tape recorder would be replaced by some newer technology).

What's the same about today's young teens is that they're still going through the early adolescent changes I've written about in the last several chapters, the same changes each of us lived through as young adolescents. Yes, the onset of puberty is a bit younger; but the young teen years are still years of upheaval, disorienting shifts, and newness. They're still years of fear and concern. They're still years of questions.

A really significant sameness is the reality of the young teen years as being years of discovery and sampling. And while the *duration* of adolescence has significantly lengthened, the *content* of adolescence still has the same primary tasks: Identity, autonomy, and affinity.

I wrote about these a bit in earlier chapters, but here's a quick reminder:

- *Identity* is asking, "Who am I?"
- *Autonomy* is asking, "How am I unique?" and, "What's the extent of my power?"
- *Affinity* is asking, "To whom and where do I belong?"

These three adolescent tasks have remained fairly consistent over the years of otherwise shifting youth culture.

What's Different?

Here's a partial list of the things that did *not* exist when I was a young teen:[1]

- Cell phones
- The Internet (including Web sites, buying stuff online, and everything else that's so completely normal today, including YouTube, Wikipedia, Google, and so many other staples of life)
- Home computers, PCs, Apple, laptops
- Text messages
- IM
- Hybrid cars
- Social networking
- "Friends with benefits"
- "Bi-curious"
- Cable TV
- Digital Video Recording (or TiVo)
- MP3s and downloadable music
- DVDs
- Hi-Def and widescreen TV

- Satellite radio
- Xboxes and Wiis and other amazing gaming systems ("Pong" was introduced when I was a young teen, and "Space Invaders" had just showed up in the commons of a local community college.)
- Email
- Spam (the email variety—we had the cat meat stuff in the can, though)
- Any kind of camera, video or still, that didn't need developing (other than Polaroids)
- Cordless phones
- Ringtones
- Call waiting and caller ID
- iChat or other video conferencing
- Snowboards and wakeboards

- Rollerblades
- An African-American president and a female secretary of state
- Starbucks
- Airport security (plus national security levels and terrorist threats)
- Internet porn
- Viagra
- Plastic soda bottles
- Cordless tools and appliances
- Game Boys (and Play-Station Portables and Nintendo DS and other handheld gaming systems)
- News—anywhere, anytime
- Seatbelt and car-seat laws
- Harry Potter
- Hip-hop
- Post-it Notes
- Self-service gas pumps
- X Games
- Energy drinks
- Home theaters
- *The Simpsons, SpongeBob, American Idol,* and a host of other dependable TV staples
- Reality TV
- Crack cocaine (and a host of more recent designer drugs)
- Minivans
- Global Positioning Systems (GPS)
- Voicemail
- Disposable cameras
- Disposable contact lenses
- The morning-after pill
- Doppler radar
- Space shuttles
- *USA Today*
- HIV/AIDS
- Paintball and Airsoft
- Laser tag
- ESPN
- MTV
- DNA fingerprinting
- Fantasy sports teams
- Cloning animals
- The Super Bowl as a kind of national holiday
- Suitcases with wheels on the bottom
- Body and face piercings (at least not commonly)
- Tattoos (on people other than bikers and carnies)
- McDonald's Playlands
- iPods
- Microwave ovens
- Pay-per-view and on-demand movies
- Easy-Mac
- Home printers, scanners, and copiers

Uh, yes, things have changed.[2] And it's important for us to remember that these changes aren't all external, nor are they insignificant. It would be easy to say that the Internet and other newer technologies merely change *how* we do things; the things we do are still the same. But this just isn't true, and it doesn't line up with what researchers are finding.

Think of it this way: When you were 13, you probably had access to an adult with a car who could drive you places when needed. (Of course, this wasn't true for everyone; but it was the norm of North America during the '60s, '70s, and '80s.) This "technology" had an impact on how you, as a 13-year-old, interacted with the world when compared to the lives of your great-grandparents who grew up in a time when driving everywhere wasn't the norm. This mobility had implications for spontaneity, for the reach of friendships (and possible friendships), for free-time options, for involvement in sports and other extracurricular activities, even for the context for schooling (as motorized vehicles meant schools didn't have to be within walking distance, which opened the doorway for more age-specific classrooms).

In the same sense, the technologies (and the nontechnological things as well) that are normative for our kids today shape their lives and experiences and behaviors and worldviews. These things change what it means to be a young teen.

I'll unpack this a bit more in a moment.

Three Epochs of Youth Culture

I also believe there's been a shift in the prioritization of those three adolescent tasks (identity, autonomy, and affinity).[3] Here's the gist of what I'm seeing.

The modern era of youth culture could be broken up into three epochs with slightly different values and issues. These shifts have been driven by a combination of factors:

- The lengthening of adolescence (and the drop in the age of the onset of puberty)

- The acceptance (or other responses) of youth culture by culture at large
- Changes in technology that have impacted relationships and other human interactions

To oversimplify things a bit (these are generalizations), we could say that the first epoch of youth culture spanned from post-World War II to about 1970; from 1970 to the millennial turn was the second epoch; and we're now in the third epoch. In each of these time periods, my contention is that the prioritization of those three adolescent tasks has shifted.

In the earliest days of modern youth culture, identity ("Who am I?") was the long leg of the three-legged stool. Youth culture was new and just beginning to gain some acceptance by culture at large. Identity trumped the other two tasks, as youth culture (if we can personify it for a moment) tried to figure out who it was.

Then at the end of the first epoch and the beginning of the second, people accepted youth culture and all the "stuff" that comes with it—norms and behaviors and attitudes, music, clothing styles, language—and youth culture shifted to a place of trying to differentiate itself from culture at large. This is the task of autonomy ("How am I different?"). You can see this most markedly in the counter-cultural youth movements of the late '60s and throughout the '70s. But I believe autonomy remained the top priority for a few decades.[4]

The third epoch arose, in a sense, because the second epoch was so successful. Youth culture (often with the help of marketers and other adults interested in getting into the minds and pockets of teenagers) continually found ways to be extremely "other" than the culture at large; at the same time, youth culture on a popular level became a dominant shaper of the adult world and the culture at large. Thus, youth culture splintered into multiple subcultures, and it went underground.[5]

This splintered and subterranean nature of today's youth culture has created a vacuum of belonging that has once again shuffled the deck of adolescent tasks. I believe affinity ("Where do I belong?") is now the long leg of the three-legged stool. It's not that identity and autonomy aren't important anymore—they are! But today's teenagers are using their desperate need for belonging as a *lens through which they address* the identity and autonomy tasks.

What does that mean for us? Well, this change in youth culture (including early adolescent culture) means that church youth ministries can't be about entertaining kids anymore. We can't just provide a middle-school-appropriate "show" for them, with neat games and a young-teen-savvy sermon. And it means that our parenting must be more engaged than ever. Our kids *need* to find a place of belonging in our homes; and they often need our help and support in finding healthy places of belonging outside our homes. Remember, their identity and autonomy will be informed by their place of belonging, so where they find belonging is critically important.

The Fabric of Culture

There are dozens of definitions for the word *culture,* as it's used by a variety of fields of knowledge. But for our purposes, this definition is helpful:

The sum total of ways of living
built up by a group of human beings
and transmitted from one generation to another.[6]

There are a few key words and phrases in that pithy little sentence:

- "Sum total": Culture is *all* the stuff we collectively do and think, the metanarrative that gives meaning and future direction to our collective story.
- "Ways of living": Culture is about how we think and live. In other words, it's not just esoteric and philosophical; culture impacts our daily lives, moment by moment. It's about what we do and why we do it.
- "Built up": Culture is created. But it's not just created by *them*; we create it together. And since we all work together to make this thing—this "way of living"—it's constantly morphing and mutating, shifting and evolving.

- "By a group of human beings": Developing cultural norms is a human enterprise. We might like to point fingers at "the media" or "marketing" and blame them for the parts of culture we don't like. However, nothing becomes a part of culture without first gaining acceptance by the populace, which, to one extent or another, includes us.
- "Transmitted from one generation to another": Dude, that last line sounds almost biblical. While culture is evolving and shifting, it's also being handed down and cross-pollinated. Culture is transmitted along parent—teen lines, as well as via peers, social networks, and other arenas of human interaction and influence.

One more important framing idea: The aspects of young teen culture that I'm going to unpack in the next section could be misunderstood as negative or as signs that humanity is on the decline. I don't write these with a "this is bad" mindset. Culture is neutral, at least in the sense that it is the real world that surrounds us, and parents are called to engage their children in their real world. Sure, there are aspects of culture that are unfortunate because they've caused kids to live in ways that aren't healthy or aren't best for their development. And there are times and reasons for us to introduce countercultural ideas and practices. But the argument over bad versus good isn't something I'm going to spend time on. I will say that I find it interesting how some adults are so willing to adopt these technologies that shape our culture while they simultaneously rip the cultural impact of those "advances." It's time for us to own our part in the evolution of culture.

Young Teen Culture

So how does all that shake down for today's middle schoolers? And what's unique or more intensified for young teens?

A Culture of Information

We all live in a culture of information. So, in a sense, this isn't unique to young teens. What is unique is that this reality is shaping them significantly during their early adolescent development and in ways that weren't true prior to the last decade. What's also unique is that today's young teens have *always* lived in a culture of information.

Almost every bit of information needed (as well as excessive quantities of information that are *not* wanted or needed) is available with the click of a mouse and in ways that shape our worldviews. This is both about access to information and the onslaught of information. The access of information shapes middle schoolers' culture of immediacy, their sense of entitlement, and their work ethic. On the other hand, the onslaught of information has a numbing effect.[7] Since everything middle schoolers need to know is readily available and since they're constantly bombarded with suggestions and data of every sort, they're less attentive to the stuff that passes by.

A Culture of Immediacy

Think for a minute about the things you had to wait for as a middle schooler that today's middle schoolers don't. They can take a picture on their cameras or cell phones and see the results instantly. They hear a song on the radio, and they can instantly download it to their computers or cell phones. Want to buy something? They can jump online in seconds, browse a customized and instantly generated list of sites, get others' input about an item via user comments, and then, if they want the item, make an instant purchase and wait a day or two at most for the item to arrive. If you've ever been "stuck" somewhere without your cell phone and tried to find a pay phone to make a call, then you've been reminded of this shift.

Sure, you and I also have access to all this immediacy. But most of us didn't grow up with this being normative. Today's young teens have never known a world without instant everything. Doesn't it strike you as funny that their idea of "old-time hominess" includes making bread in a computer-enabled machine that does all the work?

Here's a great example of this shift: For us adults, email communication changed everything. We were able to send and receive written communication without writing it by hand and going through the "hassle" of using the postal system. Written communication became almost instantaneous. But no one predicted that teenagers would dispose of email as being too slow and clunky and then opt for the intensely more immediate communication pathway of text messaging. We adults saw text messaging as a utilitarian means of quick planning. Teenagers turned it into a social phenomenon.

Middle schoolers don't have a willingness (or perhaps even the capacity) to wait for anything. Our culture has trained them to expect everything instantly. Patience is a rough one; "delayed gratification" is a foreign concept; and slowness can have a deeply profound impact on them, since it's something they simply don't experience in their everyday lives.

A Disposable Culture

Along with everything being instantly accessible, we also live in an era of disposability. Some things, such as disposable contact lenses and printer ink cartridges, are understood entirely as items to be used up and thrown away. Many more things have a sense of disposability to them, from cell phones to iPods to laptop computers. Even an MP3 file seems more disposable than a physical CD.

Just like other aspects of the middle school world, this "use it a bit, then toss it" mentality has been the norm for these kids their whole lives. So it naturally flows over into other realms of their thinking in ways that are new to this generation:

Relationships have a sense of disposability to them these days.
Knowledge has a sense of disposability to it these days.
Beliefs have a sense of disposability.
And affiliations.
And trust.
And truth.

The subconscious thinking is: If something new is going to replace this next week anyhow, why should I be attached to it now?

A Culture of Consumerism

Earlier, I noted that it's time for us adults to own our complicity in today's culture. Nowhere is this more true than with consumerism.

A significant portion of the still-forming identity of today's middle schooler is just that: "I am a consumer." They've learned this from the obvious places, such as advertisements everywhere. It's become so prevalent we may not even realize that it's not always been this way. For example, do you remember when major sports arenas weren't "sponsored"? Or the era before ad revenue was the primary fuel of the Internet? Do you remember when *product placement* was a term you didn't know?

But schooling in how to be a consumer is not just a product of those people in the marketing world. Almost everything and everyone in the lives of young teens treats them as consumers.

And treating young teens as consumers—get ready for the "ouch"—is what most of our churches and youth ministries do also. Unfortunately, I see it played out in many homes also.

Some time ago, I heard British youth leader Mike Pilavachi speak at a Youth Specialties National Youth Workers Convention. He shared the narrative of his earliest days in youth ministry, when he worked hard to provide the best "youth ministry show" in town. A turning point came for him on the night he put together a fun movie party for his group. He arranged comfortable seating, provided fun movie snacks, prepared a bit of stand-up comedy beforehand, and showed a fun film. At the end of the night, the room was trashed and all the kids were walking out. The last girl looked at the state of the room, turned to Mike, and said, "Wow, this room is a real mess." He thought she might offer to help clean it up, but instead she said, "You're really going to have to clean this up!" And then she walked out.

Mike was furious as he went about the work of cleaning up. He thought about how unappreciative the kids were, and he even thought how they "didn't deserve him." But an intrusive thought (from God, Mike was sure) came to him: Why are they this way? The only honest answer Mike could give was, I've made them this way. Mike said, "When we treat them as consumers, they play their part very well."

Or, consider this example of the consumerism perpetuated in our own homes: I was chatting with my middle school guys small group about their parents, and asked the very abstract question, "What role do your parents play in your life?" The first boy to answer smiled and said, "My parents are the people who get me stuff!"

This is one of those "less neutral" parts of middle school culture that we can work to undo. Or at least we can be intentional about not adding to it.

An Intense but Temporary Culture

In the chapter on middle school relational change (chapter 6), I wrote that young teen girl friendships are often surprisingly intense yet also tend to be short-lived. To some degree this is also true of middle school culture in general.

Some of this is developmental. In their effort to sample and discover, young teens often immerse themselves into their interests, affinity groups, or value systems. They try these on as if they're the last ones they'll ever try on, as if they're going to give their lives to this new direction.

My daughter, Liesl, who's now 16, has always been an all-or-nothing kid—and this was especially true during her young teen years. When she was into art (taking art classes and such), she was convinced she'd spend the rest of her life doing it. When she decided she wanted to be a skateboarder, she adopted everything of that subculture (including music, clothing, and many other seemingly unrelated variables) in a "this is who I am" manner. Liesl has gone through a dozen or more identity makeovers, and has only in the last year or so started to settle into some less-temporary identity wrappings.

We adults tend to either try things on more tentatively or immerse ourselves in things we will stick with for a long time. Not so, usually, with young teens. I titled this chapter "White-Hot Temporary" for this reason: Young teens give themselves wholeheartedly to the interest, relationship, choice, value system, or belief that's in their faces, but they also easily discard it for the next sampling exercise. This is a cultural issue, in addition to being a developmental issue, because it's what they observe all around them in other young teens. It's considered normal.

We adults might ask, "Why don't you ever stick with anything long enough to really know if it's you?" But their peers sure aren't saying that to them.

A Networked Culture

Obviously, this is a huge shift in young teen culture. The fact that most young teens (sure, not all of them) have cell phones that instantly connect them with parents and friends is a whole new world of instant, networked connectivity. Text messages, Facebook, Twitter, and other social networking tools have created a middle school culture that exists in bits and bytes.

This is a fascinating shift. While relationships are as important as ever, these relationships are more dependent than ever (seriously, more than ever—in all of history) on the written word. Friendships are no longer primarily dependent on physical proximity, audible vocalization, and listening. Friendships and social networks of middle schoolers are more dependent on networks played out over transmitted data.

As such, the "Who's in your network?" question of identity and affinity is more than a cell phone company marketing tag. Most young teens consider online and text communications to be both the foundations and the buttresses of their relational cathedrals.

A quick example: My daughter has a formerly very close friend who lives only about a mile away from us, but no longer attends her school. He has a cell phone, but it's almost always out of minutes (since he has a very limited prepaid plan). So she can rarely reach him by cell phone or text message. He doesn't use Facebook (which Liesl does). So even though he lives in reasonable proximity to Liesl, she's finding she has no real means of sustaining the friendship. She has other friends who no longer attend the same school she does, but she still considers them to be very close friends because they constantly—daily—connect via text messaging and Facebook (and the occasional phone call).

A Driven yet Sedentary Culture

This is an interesting, paradoxical tension among young teens today. On the one hand, the pressures on middle schoolers are greater now than they've ever been. Today's young teens are driven in ways that are almost scary. Some of this drivenness comes from their own choosing; but most of it is an external drive from parents and schools.

Not all kids play sports, of course; but for those who do, involvement in sports seems to be less about having fun and getting exercise. Instead, involvement in sports often carries with it a sense of the future: What doors will this open? Sports are seen in a utilitarian sense, as a means to get somewhere in life. In other words, the pursuit of the American dream (financial freedom and career success) is more competitive and fleeting than ever. And sports are seen as one of the many Lego pieces that will build an edge over others, increasing the likelihood of "success."

Yet sports are only one example. We see this driven reality play out in the lives of countless nonsporting middle schoolers, too. The message seems to be: *You must be the best at something if you hope to be successful in life.*

Of course, this plays out academically also. Not every kid is college-bound, but the pressure to succeed academically permeates much of teenage culture—including the culture of young teens. I'm pretty sure there was no such thing as SAT prep for middle schoolers when we were that age.

But with all this pressure and drivenness, there's an odd tension at play in the lives of young teens: They are more sedentary than ever. They don't move as much. They watch more TV, sit at computers, sit in their rooms and text their friends, and sit in front of gaming systems for hours on end.[8] The notion of a pick-up game of stickball in the street has little more than an old-timey Norman Rockwell vibe to it these days. When the young teen guys I know get together with friends, it's rarely for any kind of physical activity; young teen guys typically get together to play video games.[9]

Our Role

So what's our role in our middle schoolers' lives when it comes to culture? This is a challenging question, and it's easier to just blow it off. But parents who want to thoughtfully engage their young teens must be proactive in two ways:

We Must Be Students of Culture

It's close to impossible to be the life coaches and guide for the spiritual journeys of our children if we don't expend the effort to learn about the culture they live in. (This is similar to what I wrote earlier about how we need to learn about early adolescent developmental stuff.)

I believe this calls for a shift in parents' self-perception. For many years, parents have seen themselves primarily as disciplinarians. In more recent years, all too many parents have traded this in for the role of "friend" with their teenager. This probably has as much to do with Baby Boomer and Gen-X parents who want to hold onto their own youth. (Let's be honest and call that pretending, huh?) A youth pastor friend of mine recently accompanied a public school eighth-grade trip to Washington DC as a chaperone. The trip organizer, a teacher, was the only other adult male. But there were a host of moms on the trip as chaperones. Upon returning, my friend said to me, "If I see evidence of one more 'mom-thong,' I think I'm going to scream." Really, our kids need us to be much more than buddies or disciplinarians.

I'd like to propose a couple of new images for our role as parents: Cultural anthropologists and adventure guides. As anthropologists, we learn about the young-teen experience, we study the generalities of development and culture, and we get to know the real issues and stories of the young teens living under our roof. Then we act as their adventure guides through the early adolescent experience, including—but not limited to—their spiritual journeys.

We Must Engage in Cultural Exegesis

But we must not stop at simply being students who seek to understand culture. We must take it a step further, by engaging in cultural exegesis.

Exegesis, if you're not familiar with the word, is a fancy synonym for *interpreting.* It's usually used in the church and in connection with the act of preaching from Scripture. A preacher engages in scriptural exegesis to dig into the original intention of the passage and bring about an interpretive explanation for our context. In the same sense, we need to dig into the values and forces that shape early adolescent culture and then work as interpreters for our children.

This isn't about culture bashing. Helping young teens learn to see the good, bad, and neutral in their own culture is a huge part of good middle school parenting. And much of this can be accomplished by offering experiences that differ from what young teens experience in their everyday worlds. Two key words to think about in this area are *slow* and *quiet.*

The Dream of Culture Creation

A final idea as we're thinking about young teen culture and, specifically, the notions of culture shaping and being countercultural. Let's remember this: As followers of Jesus, we're living in the culture of the world but with a priority and allegiance to the culture of the kingdom of God.

I live for, long for, pray for, and dream of homes with middle schoolers whose families are dripping with the values of kingdom culture: Love and grace, justice and mercy, selflessness and humility, gratitude and growth.

Wow. That's quite a dream, huh?

Recently, I was asked during a magazine interview to provide "steps of discipleship" for teenagers. I'm not a big fan of a "steps" approach, because it implies that the process of following Jesus is the same for everyone or every family in every context. I believe the process of discipleship has a cultural element to it. So I said that in my response, but then I went on to say that if I must provide "steps," they would be these:

Get to know your middle schooler. (Of course you know *about* your young teen, but really get to know your son or daughter. Understand his hopes and his fears, her dreams and her stresses.)

Get to know Jesus.

Live in the way of Jesus yourself so you become a living laboratory for your own reflection and for your son or daughter to observe.

Exercise prayerful discernment *with* your son or daughter about what an approach to discipleship should look like in your home.

Try something. Live a life of faith in action together.

That, friends, is what it means for us to live into the dream of a kingdom-of-God culture for our homes.

A FEW WORDS TO PARENTS

PRESSURE TO PERFORM

Bella is a wildly capable early teen. She's wickedly smart, plays club soccer, serves at church, is a great big sister, and loves her friends. Bella's also surrounded by incredibly loving parents and has a few adult leaders who pour into her life. She has big dreams for her future, and I don't doubt she'll achieve whatever she attempts. To every onlooker, Bella's got it all together and has an incredibly promising future.

But recently, during her eighth-grade rite-of-passage ceremony, Bella broke down. Even with all the support and love from her parents and community, the pressure to perform overwhelms her. She wonders who will love her the first time she fails big time. She fears what will happen if she lets them down. She questions how long she can keep up her perfect performance. Bella opened up about how much stress she feels balancing school, sports, family, friends, and church. With tears streaming down her face, and her mom curling up next to her on the carpet, she vulnerably confessed that she can't do it all, but she feels like she has to. After all, "College is only four years down the road." She's forced to start making decisions yesterday about high school classes that will affect her SAT scores, college admissions, and future job. Bella is 13 years old.

Only a couple of generations ago, young teens didn't have to face the kinds of decisions they face today. When I was a junior higher, in the early '90s, I never stressed about college and career the way my students do today. The same is probably true of you and your generation. I consistently hear from young teens that they feel a great deal of pressure to get the grades, keep the grades, do the extracurricular activities that will look good on the college résumé, be an outstanding citizen, and do it all while smiling.

Parents, plus a team of other adults, have to care about a middle schooler's whole life, regardless of his or her performance. I've come to understand that parents and other adults must provide support—scaffolding, really—around students. Kids need the assurance that when they fail, mess up, or express doubt, they will still have caring adults in their corner, regardless of their GPAs, extracurricular activities, or how "good" they are. And as a culture, I believe we must rethink how much pressure we put on our young teens. Is the pressure to excel worth it, if it's causing kids like Bella so much stress? Will it be worth it if a generation of kids like Bella gain the whole world, but lose their souls?

*−April L. Diaz is the NextGen pastor
at New Song Church in Irvine, California.*

Chapter 10

The Overlapping Transition

(A Few More Implications)

Do you remember the video game *Frogger?* (Stick with me, even if you have no clue what I'm talking about.) To play it, you control a little frog that tries to cross a street or a river. You could move the frog to the left and right, forward and backward. On the street levels of the game, the goal was to jump from the safety of the starting curb and across lanes of traffic by hopping into the spaces between the cars and trucks as they drive by. And there was a median in the middle of the screen where the frog could rest before hopping through the traffic going in the other direction. On the river levels, the goal was still to cross over successfully, but to do so you had to jump onto the moving turtles, logs, and lily pads before they sank.

In both cases, the overall objective was the same: Leave the safety of one curb or shore, navigate the potentially life-ending obstacles of the transitional space, and—hopefully—arrive at the safety of the far curb or shore.[1]

For many years I thought of the middle school experience this way. In my mind's eye, I pictured preteens ambling up to the shore of a turbulent river. Then at puberty, I pictured them wading into the swirling shallows and eventually moving out to depths beyond their ability to stand as they battled the currents, waves, and eddies of early adolescence.

Then as they moved into the middle teen or high school years, I pictured them safely arriving at some kind of distant shore. What, exactly, that far shore was didn't really factor into this metaphor too much. (Maybe it was just the median?)

But after many years spent working with thousands of middle schoolers, I've come to see this metaphor as flawed. The "Frogger Transition"—or any metaphor that portrays young teens leaving safety, moving into a transitionary space, and arriving at some kind of post-transitionary space—is not the experience of real middle school kids. Instead, early adolescence is an *overlapping* transition. The transitional space in the middle is "both–and," rather than being "no longer–not yet."

In other words, young teens move into a transitional period in which they are still children in many ways—holding cautiously to childhood ideas and conclusions, finding safety and comfort in childhood toys and fantasies, retreating to spaces that are known. But at the same time, they're fully experimenting with the world of adolescence and adulthood: Trying on new behaviors and values like clothes on a rack, sampling attitudes and ideas, testing the waters of doubt and questioning.

We might think of this, in metaphorical terms, as the blending between colors.[2] Since this book is printed in black on white, we'll use a grayscale. But the metaphor works with any blending of two colors. Using this metaphor, middle school is gray. It's an overlapping or blending of the childhood and adolescent life stages.

The young teen experience is not this:

And it's not this:

Instead, the young teen experience is this:

There's a sense of advance and retreat during this process, but it's not as clean as "two steps forward and one step back." Sometimes young teens take one step forward and two steps back. But just as often, they'll take one step forward and then quickly take one step back. And once in a while they'll take two steps forward and no steps back. There's no predicting this at a micro level, and the whole process of moving from childhood to full-on teenagerhood can only be seen at a macro level, from a satellite view.

Barbie Dolls and Punk Pokémons

Let's look at a couple of real examples to flesh this out a bit.

The first example involves a girl who was part of my middle school ministry a few years ago. I'm sure you know girls just like this (maybe even in your own home!), as I've seen lots of them in my ministries. Marcie was 12 years old and in seventh grade. She was ahead of the curve in her physical development. She could have easily passed for a 16-year-old. She was pretty, and she knew how to work that. Marcie had perfectly styled hair that wasn't one bit teenybopper, and she had fingernails that made all the women in our ministry jealous. Marcie knew how to wear makeup tastefully (unlike some young teen girls who look as though they're heading for careers in street walking or theater).

Marcie was also relationally mature, and she was comfortable and at ease in adult conversation. Adult leaders liked being around Marcie because she made them feel comfortable, almost as though they were chatting with a peer.

Pretty much everything about Marcie made her seem mature beyond her years—except Marcie was still totally into Barbie dolls. At an age when almost every other girl had *long since* discarded her dolls or forgotten them in the back of a closet or sold them on eBay, Marcie loved her dolls.

And this wasn't the semi-acceptable Barbie affection of an adult collector. Marcie didn't value her Barbies for their monetary worth; Marcie loved her Barbie dolls as childhood playthings. She'd regularly bring a Barbie or two on overnight trips with the youth group, and they could be found resting on her pillow during nonsleeping hours. Some kids teased her about this, but Marcie wasn't emotionally perceptive enough to realize it was teasing. She believed the other kids thought her Barbies were fun. And she regularly mistook their play-along mocking as genuine interest in her dolls.

Marcie was in the midst of this overlapping transition. She was still a child in some ways, but she was already an emerging young woman in many other ways. Both-and.

Then there were the guys I called "The Punk Pokémons." (I never called them that to their faces, of course.) You've seen wolf packs of guys like this, I'm sure.

The Punk Pokémons were an affinity group of about five guys who were always present at our middle school ministry, but never fully engaged. (Full engagement was contrary to the accepted norms of their group, after all.) They were in eighth grade, and they were all taller than I was. They wore all black, and they always slumped down in their chairs in the back row with their arms crossed and an "I dare you to try to interest me" look on their faces. Seriously, they were an intimidating lot with a constant façade of boredom and seething anger.

In those rare instances when they used words (they typically used grunts and other sounds more often than actual words), the PPs (ha!) would respond with one-word answers. They never initiated conversation unless it was to tell leaders that something was stupid. They all listened to old-skool punk music, and they were committed to a simplistic, childish concept of what anarchy might mean.

But they were all seriously into trading Pokémon cards. (This was a few years back, when Pokémon cards—those cute little Japanese anime trading cards—were the rage.) The PPs would huddle in a back corner of our middle school room, all brooding and quiet, and it looked as though they were in the midst of a drug trade, or plotting the overthrow of the world. But if one got close enough, one could just barely overhear a plea like, "I'll trade you two Pikachus for that Mewtwo!"

The Punk Pokémons were living large in the turbulent transitional waters of early adolescence. Certainly, within a year or two, most of them would leave behind their Pokémon card collections in favor of more fully teenage interests and pursuits. But, for now, they were blissfully unaware of the incongruence of this holdover from their childhoods with everything else in their carefully manicured affinity group norms.

How Should We Respond?

I've written this multiple times already, but it bears repeating in the context of this discussion of transition. Our role is to serve as grace-filled tour guides on the journey of early adolescence. This has a few practical applications:

1. **Never try to rush or push your son or daughter into adolescence.** We show them grace by loving them in the midst of this weirdness. If you notice that your middle school son has a stuffed animal on his bed, realize that you are on very thin ice. If you make a joke about it, you might "help" him discard this childhood holdover; but you're likely crushing one of the few safe zones he has in his otherwise upside-down and all-changing world. A little joke, no matter how unintentional, can completely destroy a kid—and damage your influence on his life.

2. **To the extent you are able, protect your child from teasing (or, at least be super-engaged when it happens).** Sooner or later, Marcie will discover that the other kids were actually teasing her. And the realization that they've been teasing her all along will likely hit her like a tidal wave. She'll probably feel tiny and stupid, and she'll most likely experience betrayal. Be her ally in this, encouraging her, normalizing her experience, and standing with Marcie if and when this realization does occur. You'll likely not be present when the teasing occurs, but you can look for signs of it, even if she doesn't choose to reveal it on her own. For example, if Marcie suddenly packs up all her Barbie dolls and stuffs them in the back of her closet, you might ask about her reasons, providing love and grace and a listening ear, not diminishing her pain but being present to her in the midst of it. Marcie will gradually move on from her Barbie dolls, and the PPs will lose interest in their trading cards. And hopefully this will occur naturally and without trauma and drama. There are enough opportunities for feeling stupid and outside the norm in middle school, so try to minimize those experiences in your home.

3. **Walk alongside your son or daughter.** Whatever metaphor you choose for the turbulent transition of middle school, it's messy. And good parents of young teens will get some of this mess on them.

If we're using the river-crossing metaphor, we can't just stand on either shore (the "sending shore" or the "receiving shore") and shout out instructions and encouragement. We must get in and dog-paddle alongside our teens. Hopefully, you've learned enough about the currents and obstacles that you can act as a river guide, providing some orientation, close-up encouragement, and the occasional lifeline. And if we're using the color blend metaphor, we become color consultants, palette guides, art coaches.

That Satellite View

In addition to being in the midst of things with our middle schoolers, we need to have that big picture view I referred to earlier. We have an understanding of what's going on in their lives; we have a sense of where they're headed; we have ideas about how their choices will impact them.

And, most importantly, we have a confidence about what God is doing in their lives.

We don't offer young teens our perspectives in condescending ways. ("You need to grow up!" "Why would you make that choice? Can't you see where it will lead?") We don't offer our perspective in a distant and removed way, shouting down on them from a metaphorical megaphone. And we don't pretend to know it all or to have all the answers or to have everything figured out in our own lives.

Instead, our perspective and involvement is that we *have seen* the situation from our satellite viewpoint, but we're now journeying with and alongside our middle school children. We have both understanding and experiences (our own and what we've observed in others) that are valuable, necessary, and helpful. But we bring that understanding and perspective just as Christ brought his to us: We live incarnationally alongside our children—not merely as buddies or disciplinarians, but as relationally engaged and loving guides.

A FEW WORDS TO PARENTS

ENJOY THE JOURNEY

Every other summer while I was growing up, we made the trip from Chicago to Maine in our family van. My parents were so determined to get their three rambunctious sons to Grandpa and Grandma's house that we always took the fastest and most direct route. It wasn't until college that I discovered the quaint villages of Maine's coast and ate my first fresh lobster.

Unfortunately, the world has the same kind of itinerary for our middle schoolers. Our young teens are being pushed to their final destination (adulthood) so quickly that we often forget to look around and enjoy the journey with them. There are more than a few books that tell parents how to "survive" their child's middle school years. They seem to advocate burying our heads in the sand until our kids get through this unfortunate stage and return to their sweet and compliant natures.

But what if, by wishing away the middle school years, we are missing out on God's reminder of the wonder and passion and heartache and struggle that is the Christian faith? We need middle schoolers' voices as interpreters of the faith. They approach life and faith with a great curiosity. They are deciphering clues about who they are and what life is all about. They are asking questions that adults have given up on a long time ago. They are looking for different things than adults, and they see things we are quick to dismiss. We need their idealism to keep us from souring into cynicism. We need their experimentation and wonder to inspire us to take risks in pursuit of something new. We must tap into the extravagant quantities of passion that allow them to throw off all inhibition and worship like no other human being can.

Actually, traveling the coast of Maine is a lot like middle school ministry: the journey seems endless, the smells are a little funky, but the views are breathtaking. It's for this reason I love taking parents on our ministry's retreats and mission projects. Having parents walk and work alongside middle schoolers is an exciting win for the family, the middle school ministry, and the entire church. It's breathtaking to be with parents as they witness the amazing God-sightings that happen in the lives of their middle schoolers. Most importantly, it is a great reminder that we in the church must never forsake our first love (Revelation 2:4). Any time spent around middle schoolers is an opportunity to fall back in love with the God who was crazy in love with us as middle schoolers, and still loves us today.

*—Andy Jack is the middle school pastor
at Christ Church of Oak Brook in Oak Brook, Illinois.*

My Prayer for You

I began this book by stating that the young teen years are one of the most misunderstood and underappreciated developmental periods of human life. I hope that after reading these pages your awareness and appreciation for the uniqueness of the middle schooler in your own home has grown, and many of your apprehensions about parenting him or her have lessened. I pray that some experiences and perspectives from my own sometimes-bumbling attempts to serve this classically awkward age group (in churches, and with my own two kids) have helped you look at your young teen with new eyes.

But I pray for more than that. Much more.

Because somewhere, in a place far from me, but very close to you, lives a young teen:

A very specific young teen.

A young teen who desperately wants someone to know his fears, his hopes, his story.

A middle schooler with a head full of particular worries, and insecurities, and wonderings.

A kid who's trying to understand her parents, the opposite sex, and where tears come from.

A person who's discovering new facets in the drama of friendship-making. And friendship-losing, too.

A middle schooler frustrated by acne, inclined to frequent goofiness, loved by Jesus.

I don't know that specific young teen.

But you do!

You see, my prayer isn't just that you become smarter or more informed about young teens in general—or even that you've picked up a few new ideas or strategies.

I pray that you see yourself as even more "use-able" in the life of that one young teen—your son, your daughter. What a gift (to you, and to your child).

I pray that you're ready to keep investing, keep listening, keep asking questions, keep praying.

I pray you realize that a moment is never wasted when you're engaged in the life of your child—when you're being with them.

Sharing the love of Jesus Christ…and sharing life together, too.

> *Because we loved you so much,*
> *we were delighted to share with you*
> *not only the gospel of God*
> *but our lives as well.*

1 Thessalonians 2:8

With much love from a fellow traveler on this wonderful journey of parenting a young teen,

Marko

See Jane Face New Issues

by Dr. Kara Powell and Brad Griffin

See Jane.[1]
    See Jane thrive in elementary school.
    See Jane enter middle school.
    See Jane face new issues—different issues than the Janes of the 1980s or 1990s.
    See Jane struggle.
    See Jane grow.
    While middle school has always been a time of developmental change, girls today face new issues, as well as new twists on not-so-new issues. As we youth workers hustle to keep up with all that Jane (or Juanita or Janesha or Jin-Ha) faces, we're grateful for a recent batch of research that helps us better understand the paths our middle school girls must navigate. We hope these insights will help you parents as you seek to walk alongside your young teen daughters as they tread new paths.

See Jane Cyber-Pioneer

Online Creativity

At age 14, Ashley Qualls built a million-dollar Web enterprise from her room.
    Yes, at age 14.
    And, yes, from her room.
    By creating online page designs and offering them via her Web site, whateverlife.com (which now draws 250,000 unique visitors—mostly teen girls—each day), Ashley quickly became the young-teen

CEO of a booming online venture. The MySpace page designs are free; the money comes via advertisers who line up to buy a spot on Ashley's site.

Ashley is a prototype of the new tech-savvy teen girl. And she's not alone—either in her success or her tech savvy. When she launched a magazine to get more girls interested in creating Web content, a thousand teens quickly volunteered to contribute.

Text-Fest

Undoubtedly you've already observed that text messaging is vastly changing the way middle school girls (and guys, of course) communicate. The pace is nothing less than breathtaking. Teen girls now report spending more time texting than talking on their cell phones—and the top reason for this is so they can multitask. Forty percent of teens say they would "die" if they couldn't text on their phone, and 45 percent agree that their cell phones are key to their social lives.[2]

Jane can be in touch with her friends anywhere, anytime, and in short bursts of gossip, affirmation, insult, or inspiration. Whether caught in a social setting where she feels unsafe, stuck alone in her room, or even—ugh—with her family, today's Jane can find instant relational salvation via her trusty cell phone.

How Can We Respond?

Connect with Our Daughters via Text

For the young teen girls in our homes, an inbox with one new text sends the message that someone cares. Since teenagers use texting more as a means of social connection than information transmittal (the latter is the more dominant use of texting for adults), there's great opportunity for parents to connect with their daughters if the parents occasionally stop to "think like a teenage girl" and connect via text. Ask for prayer, send quick notes of affirmation, and even tee up deep conversations you can pick up face-to-face. Texts can also contribute to lighthearted fun in your family, like sending a goofy photo to your daughter attached to a text. Sure, she might roll her eyes and tell her friends how weird her parents are; but that's usually the outward response only—inwardly, you're paving the way for a relationship that's not only about discipline and rules.

Crossing the Line

In the midst of Jane's navigation of new technology, she needs parents to help her think through what she should be sharing publicly and what she should consider keeping private (such as photos of herself nude or in her underwear, to name one of the most rampant and troubling trends). Online boundaries are nebulous, and girls need parents, and other caring adults, to help them navigate the flood of possibilities that await them as they learn to express themselves digitally.

One middle school girl from our church received a text in which a friend declared (for the first time) that she was gay. Interestingly, the girl from our church wasn't at all surprised to learn her friend's news through a text, but I'm so glad she shared the text with her small group leader who could help her explore the feelings this news generated.

Mom, Can't It Wait?

We also have the chance to directly address the issue of multitasking and the ways texting feeds into that practice. We can help our daughters process the pros and cons of multitasking when it includes things like texting while simultaneously talking to other people (or God), and help them understand the frustration other people (of all ages!) experience when a conversation is interrupted by texting.

To Text or Not to Text?

Having said that, we also need to develop a healthy set of guidelines for our daughters when it comes to texting—including boundaries for how we, as parents, use texting with our own children. You may disagree, but our opinion is that unlimited texting plans aren't necessary, and that a middle school girl learning to monitor and limit her texting quantity is a healthy thing.

Also think about how you model those same boundaries. Ask yourself: Where do I draw my texting boundaries? Do I ever look at my phone or send a text when my daughter is talking to me? How often do I participate in texting conversations that go on, and on, and on? When do I need to shut down the finger punching and choose either a vocal conversation or (dare we suggest) silence?

The middle school "culture of immediacy" (see chapter 9) assumes instant responses, always, to texts. There is great value in showing that you have boundaries and cannot (or choose not to) always respond immediately.

Phones: Away or Not?

It's also very legitimate—even highly recommended—to have family boundaries as to when everyone can or cannot use their phones. The challenge is: This can't be a double standard; you have to keep the agreed boundaries also. If you set a standard that no one will answer cell phones or even look at them during family meals (a great idea, by the way), you quickly become a hypocrite if you answer your phone and say, "But that was a really important call." To the mind of a middle school girl, her calls and texts are just as important as yours.

See Jane Try to Be Sexy

The Damage Done

Those of us who care about middle school girls have intuitively sensed that pressure to be "sexy" damages the way they view themselves and others. A 2007 report by the American Psychological Association spells out the destruction more explicitly. Whether it's a five-year-old girl walking through a shopping mall in a short T-shirt that says JUICY or a magazine article that promises teenage girls that losing 10 pounds will get them the boyfriend of their dreams, sexualization is linked to impaired cognitive performance, eating disorders, low self-esteem, and even physical health problems.[3]

The Parent Trap

More than 77,000 invasive cosmetic surgical procedures are performed on teens (middle and high school students) each year.[4]

While that is shocking in and of itself, consider this: Minors cannot undergo these surgeries without their parents' consent. Plus, since most of these procedures are not covered by medical insurance, parents usually pay for the surgery as well.

Mom–Daughter Competition

Much attention has been placed on the messages that the media sends to young girls about their bodies, and rightly so. But what about the messages from Mom? More and more moms seem to be competing with their teenage daughters for the perfect body and wearing clothes that show off their efforts. Girls are struggling to keep up. With bodies that change faster than they can handle, and certainly more unpredictably than their mothers', middle school girls may find themselves in a losing race to be "sexier" than Mom.

One girl in our ministry seemed to throw in the towel during such a competition. Like her incredibly thin mom, this girl had been an avid runner and healthy eater in sixth and seventh grade. All that changed in eighth grade when the girl got curves. Her mom still runs and wears spaghetti-strap dresses, but the girl seems to be coping by eating potato chips and covering her body with baggy sweatshirts.

How Can We Respond?

No Guys Allowed

Moms can schedule a girls-only getaway with their daughters, and invite other moms and girls (and other adult female mentors) to attend. Do something fun together, but also plan some intentional discussions about body image and sexuality. Help the adults prepare ahead of time, asking them to bring a willingness to share openly and honestly about their own struggles (which will invite the same from the middle school girls).

Dear Diary...

If your middle school girl is ready to think more deeply, give her a notebook and some art supplies so she can create her own journal to help her reflect on the pressure to be sexy (Ideally, you—Mom—would create your own also). After a few weeks or months, have a check-in lunch and ask her to look back through her journal (and yours), identifying common words and themes that you can discuss together. By teaching middle school girls to journal and name forces like "pressure," "image management," and "sexualization," we're giving them lenses through which they can view, interpret, and process their experiences and feelings. Simply being able to name their experiences can help young teenagers make sense out of what otherwise feels like chaos.

At our last middle school camp, we gave our girls a bunch of watercolor paints and pens and invited them to compare the media's view of who they are with who they really are. Girls insightfully wrote comments such as, "Go Get Perfect…And Then Come Back" and "What If You Don't Have the Right Shoes?" One girl who seemed especially glad to express her feelings wrote the following anonymous poem:

Fame
Everybody wants fame.
Some use it just to look lame.
Fame or money can tear you up.
Stay in school
Keep your grades up.
Don't be foolish.
Look around.
See how Britney Spears turned upside down.
You can use Maybelline
But that can't show the inner queen.
Be who you are.

See Jane Play; See Jane Sit
The Couch Potato-Ette
There's mixed news about girls' physical activity these days. While more girls (middle school and high school) than ever are playing organized sports, overall they're becoming less active and less healthy. (Yes, even those who play a sport.) Outside of organized sports, girls

seem to be sitting around (literally) a whole lot more than they used to. Girls lag behind boys in meeting age-appropriate levels of healthy physical activity, and they drop out of organized sports more often, especially as they transition from childhood to adolescence.[5]

How Can We Respond?

Women Power

As with all things "girl," the power of the modeling of other women cannot be underestimated. And that modeling starts at home with moms and step-moms. If we moms never exercise, how can we expect our daughters to? If our typical lunch is tortilla chips and a Diet Coke, why would our daughter take the time to make a decent sandwich?

Here's an even deeper question: When our daughters do see us exercising or making nutritious food choices, what comments have we made either directly to them or around them that explain why we're doing so? Have we said we want to go to the gym because summer's coming and we want to look good in a bathing suit? Or have we explained we carve out time to work out because it helps us relieve stress and take care of the bodies God has given us? We might be doing more harm than good if our daughters think we care for our own bodies simply because we want others to notice our flatter stomachs or thinner thighs.

Non-Jocks Welcome

If your daughter doesn't play after-school sports and "hates P.E.," think of other ways you might sneak a bit more physical activity into her life. Can you buy her a pedometer and challenge her to hit 8,000 steps the next time you drop her off at the mall? Can you offer to drive her one way to a friend's house but tell her she'll have to walk home on her own? Would she enjoy a class at the gym with you as special mother/daughter time, especially if some other girl/mom pairs came along also? Your daughter will be better off not just physically but also emotionally, mentally, and maybe even socially if you can find creative ways to keep her moving.

See Jane Buy…and Feel Bad about Herself

I Feel Bad…I Want a New Shirt

Okay, it's no shock that girls are a huge consumer market. But recent research shows another twist: Teen materialism has been linked directly to self-esteem—especially among younger teens, and especially among girls. When self-esteem drops (particularly in middle school), materialism skyrockets. When self-esteem rises, materialism drops—again, especially during early adolescence. Unfortunately, self-esteem usually doesn't begin to rise again until high school.[6]

Fashion Bullying?

Young teen girls who make the "wrong" fashion purchases are in a new kind of trouble. While "fashion bullying" (meaning picking on girls because of the clothing they wear) has been going on for decades, lately psychologists and school guidance counselors have noted a new level of intensity. The middle school hall has become a bloody corral for the fashion posse. One researcher studying teen behavior in more than 20 states says she's seen a stark increase in bullying related to clothes over the past few years, alongside an increase in high-end designers targeting girls in their early teens.[7]

How Can We Respond?

More than Kitchen and Kids

Give girls opportunities to increase their self-esteem by helping them identify and use their natural and spiritual gifts. Do young teen girls experience themselves in your home and church as more than just a room cleaner, kitchen helper, or a nursery worker? If not, brainstorm with your daughter to think of ways she can meaningfully contribute to family goals, as well as to your church and community.

Help Jane Figure Out What She Actually Likes

One small group leader told us she's on a mission to take middle school girls shopping and help them think about what they're drawn to and why. She's found that most girls in her small group like a particular bathing suit or purse because of its label or the store it comes from, not because of what it actually looks like or how it's made. So she takes girls to the mall and asks girls to explain why they like what they like. Some of them never get past "because it's cool," but other girls are starting to see that there's more to style than clothing labels. This would be a fantastic mother/daughter exercise, but it would be critical that you adopt a learner posture, not a posture of condemnation or dismissal.

Teach Girls How to Advocate

A few years ago a group of 13-to-16-year-old girls was able to convince Abercrombie and Fitch to pull a line of T-shirts boasting slogans such as WHO NEEDS BRAINS WHEN YOU HAVE THESE? across the chest. Their "girlcott" is only one of a number of successful examples of girls advocating for the reduction of cultural sexualization of women.[8] What "campaigns" (even if it's a mini secret campaign between you and your daughter!) can you cook up together?

See Jane Soar

Are some of the challenges young teen girls face in this new era downright scary? You bet.

Should we fatalistically throw up our hands in surrender? Not a chance.

One of our colleagues at the Fuller Youth Institute, Dr. Desiree Segura-April, has focused much of her research on studying girls around the world. Across the globe girls face unique struggles including slavery, sex trafficking, and fewer opportunities to receive health care and education.

Yet girls around the world, especially if given a bit of nurture and support, are also often the most productive and engaged leaders. Some international leaders are advocating and ministering more to girls than boys because they see the influence Jane has in India, Zimbabwe, and Brazil. As a way of exploring these issues, we'd encourage parents and their daughters to read, together, Nicholas Kristof and Sheryl WuDunn's amazing book, *Half the Sky: Turning Oppression into Opportunity for Women Worldwide* (Vintage, 2010), and talk about the potential of women and girls.

What does it take to see Jane reach her kingdom potential? It takes courageous parents who are willing to link arms with courageous young teen girls. As we strategically respond to these new realities that our middle school girls face, we will see Jane soar.

Kara E. Powell, PhD, is a former young teen girl who now serves as a faculty member at Fuller Seminary and the executive director of the Fuller Youth Institute (www.fulleryouthinstitute.org).

Brad M. Griffin serves as the associate director of the Fuller Youth Institute (www.fulleryouthinstitute.org) and volunteers with middle school kids at his church. He was never a young teen girl, but he unsuccessfully pursued a lot of them as a young teen guy.

ENDNOTES

Introduction

1. I'll write about this quite a bit more in chapters to come. But for now, be aware that in the early 1970s, puberty began, on average, at about 13 years old; but now puberty begins, on average, at about 11 years old.
2. The ultimate "first" being birth to two years old.
3. Sometimes this age group is referred to as "tweeners" or "tweenagers."

Chapter 1

1. These rites of passage still exist in more "protected" cultures (those without access to the influence of media or a world youth culture, like tribal cultures). And ghosts of them still exist in some cultures, such as the bar mitzvah and bat mitzvah in Jewish culture. In recent years, many people have sounded the call for a return to these practices. Creating "rites of passage" can be wonderfully helpful as a marker in adolescent growth, but they'll never again be what they once were, since they're no longer a cultural norm. And new rites—while wonderful, and something I would highly encourage—should be seen as onramps, not as the adult freeway itself.
2. In 1904, G. Stanley Hall was the first to popularize the word *adolescence* (although he didn't create it) with the publication of his book by the same title (*Adolescence: Its Psychology and Its Relations to Physiology, Anthropology, Sociology, Sex, Crime, and Religion* [New York: Appleton, 1904]). Even then, Hall recognized the upper end of adolescence (then described as about 16 years old) in these terms.
3. I unpack these adolescent tasks in much more detail in my book *Youth Ministry 3.0* (Youth Specialties, 2008).
4. Researchers who study the onset of puberty pretty much always study girls. There are a couple reasons for this. First, while girls officially show signs of puberty with the growth of breast buds and pubic hair, menarche (their first period) is a widely accepted marker. These markers are all visible. And girls—throughout the ages—have been willing to talk

about their first period (at least with someone they trust). The start of puberty for boys is less obvious and less agreed upon. Some say it's a boy's first nocturnal emission. Other people have other definitions. Either way, boys don't talk about it. In fact, boys lie about it. So researchers study girls. We do know that boys tend to follow about 12 to 18 months behind girls on puberty and other adolescent development realities.

5. As college students and young adults move into a world where they have less spending power than their parents, it's common for them to experience an ambivalence about fully engaging the world as adults. They often don't have the spending power they'd like to have, and they find it difficult to imagine a life of complete independence from their parents.

6. As youth culture grew to the point of being the dominant pop culture in the Western world, it became more and more acceptable for twentysomethings to be living a life of prolonged adolescence. A 24-year-old living at home in 1968 would have been considered a slacker or to have some sort of significant problem. But a 24-year-old living at home today is rather normal. In our increasingly complex world, we no longer expect high school graduates to have figured out the questions of Identity, Autonomy, and Affinity. Culturally, we've grown to accept that young twentysomethings still "deserve" more years to wrestle with these tasks.

7. With culture change has come a prolonging of many of the physiological aspects assumed to be normal in teen years. For instance, development of abstract thinking has been shown to be slowing, lengthening well into the twenties. New brain research is also showing that parts of the brain aren't fully formed until the mid-twenties, like the prefrontal cortex and the temporal lobes. These parts of the brain are vital to functioning "as an adult." There remains debate as to whether these "not yet ready" brain functions are the chicken or the egg. In other words, it's not clear if this is how brains have always developed (and our understanding of adolescence is just now catching up), or if brain development has slowed because our culture doesn't expect teenagers to use those parts of the brain. Either way, the brain has been shown to be decidedly "teenage" well into the twenties. For more discussion of this—particularly as it pertains to brain development—see Barbara Strauch's excellent book *The Primal Teen* (Anchor, 2004).

8. This number is hotly debated. I find it intriguing that people get so passionate about disagreeing with the research on this. Really, the tone of voice when people express their skepticism can only be described as "threatened." I'm not completely sure what they're threatened by. A generous possibility is that they're hoping to protect the childhood years from being absorbed into adolescence (a trend that—puberty aside— seems to be propelled by marketing to preteens and "tweens"). When I

cite these numbers, I'm often asked (sometimes by a skeptic, sometimes by someone who's merely interested and not disagreeing) for references to studies backing this up. While I've included these endnotes, this book is certainly not a truly academic book (duh!), and I'll not fully support my claim other than to say the numbers have been shown over and over again in various studies. I will cite a few of them, if merely to allow us to move on:

Marcia E. Herman-Giddens, Eric J. Slora, Richard C. Wasserman, Carlos J. Bourdony, Manju V. Bhapkar, Gary G. Koch, and Cynthia M. Hasemeier. "Secondary Sexual Characteristics and Menses in Young Girls Seen in Office Practice: A Study from the Pediatric Research in Office Settings Network," *Pediatrics* 99, (April 1997): 505–512. http://pediatrics.aappublications.org/cgi/content/abstract/99/4/505 (accessed 3/13/09).

Diana Zuckerman Ph.D., "When Little Girls Become Women: Early Onset of Puberty in Girls," National Research Center for Women and Families—Children's Health, http://www.center4research.org/children11.html (accessed 3/13/09).

P.B. Kaplowitz, S.E. Oberfield, and the Drug and Therapeutics and Executive Committees of the Lawson Wilkins Pediatric Endocrine Society, "Reexamination of the Age Limit for Defining When Puberty is Precocious in Girls in the United States," *Pediatrics* 104, (October 1999): 936–941. http://pediatrics.aappublications.org/cgi/content/full/104/4/936?ijkey=51a3e30c7ef66356541e2f346991c5cc9300baf7 (accessed 3/13/09).

9. For more on this, see Chap Clark, *Hurt: Inside the World of Today's Teenagers* (Baker Academic, 2004), as well as Chap Clark and Dee Clark, *Disconnected: Parenting Teens in a MySpace World* (Baker Books, 2007).

10. See Barna's article on age of conversion: http://www.barna.org/barna-update/article/5-barna-update/196-evangelism-is-most-effective-among-kids (accessed 4/8/09).

11. The research of Christian Smith, referenced later in this book, is just one of the many places where this fact has been revealed.

Chapter 2

1. I searched online and in some of Stephen Glenn's books, but I couldn't find this exact description in print anywhere. So I asked Wayne Rice, the godfather of middle school ministry and author of the seminal book, *Junior High Ministry* (Zondervan/Youth Specialties, 1998), where I could find it. Here's Wayne's email response: "I'm not sure Steve ever wrote it in a book . . . maybe he did, but I remember it mainly from lectures he gave, first in a seminar called "Developing Capable People"

and then at a "trainer of trainers" seminar that [Youth Specialties] did with him in San Diego a long time ago. We also had him speak at a couple of conventions . . . I'm sure I had the little discovery-testing-concluding cycle thing in my notes from his talks. I can still see him drawing PUBERTY in big letters with lightning bolts, sort of like Emeril's 'BAM!' He'd shout, 'PUBERTY! . . . when massive doses of progesterone and testosterone come roaring into the body setting off a biophysical disaster of unprecedented proportions!'" For a more recent description of these changes, check out Stephen Glenn's foreword for *Positive Discipline for Teenagers* by Jane Nelson and Lynn Lott (Three Rivers Press, 2000).

2. I've adjusted Stephen Glenn's age brackets on this chart, to reflect the shifting age of puberty and the cultural shifts in the length of adolescence. I've also changed his word *discovery* to *sampling*, as I believe it's a more up-to-date descriptor of both the infant stage and of early adolescence.

3. I'm borrowing this metaphor from Brian McLaren, who uses it for a completely different application in some of his writings. (Brian uses it to talk about the current American church, with all its technology and meganess, which, he suggests, will continue on for some period of time, even while the new-era-automobile of churches spring up around them.)

Chapter 3

1. See the Wikipedia article on puberty: http://en.wikipedia.org/wiki/Puberty (accessed 4/8/09).

2. For more on the technicalities of menstruation, the Wikipedia article is concise and helpful: http://en.wikipedia.org/wiki/Menstruation (accessed 3/13/09).

3. James Dobson, *Preparing for Adolescence* (Regal, 1989), 83-84.

4. For a much more detailed (and helpful!) discussion about masturbation in boys, see pages 66-71 in Steve Gerali's excellent book, *Teenage Guys: Exploring Issues Adolescent Guys Face and Strategies to Help Them* (Zondervan/Youth Specialties, 2006).

5. I've already written about how adolescence has gone from an 18-month window (when it was first identified in 1904), to a 6-year window (in the 1970s), to a window of 15 years or more. But recently I read new research that proposed that adolescence should no longer be bracketed as an age, that the "age limits" of adolescence are going by the wayside, as people in their late twenties and early thirties are living a sort of extended adolescence (referred to in this research as "the golden years of adolescence," which is somewhat humorous). This is fascinating stuff to me, and it will have huge implications for youth ministry and parenting in the years to come. Here's the URL to the research I'm talking about: http://www.

marketingvox.com/youth-no-longer-defined-by-age-consumers-stay-younger-longer-041658/?camp=rssfeed&src=mv&type=textlink (accessed 3/13/09).

6. Read more about Bar Mitzvah and Bat Mitzvah rites of passage on Wikipedia, at: http://en.wikipedia.org/wiki/Bar_Mitzvah (accessed 3/13/09).

7. Read more about the Quinceañera tradition on Wikipedia, at: http://en.wikipedia.org/wiki/Quincea%C3%B1era (accessed 3/13/09).

8. Many teenagers will still say the real rite of passage is an adolescent's first sexual experience, which is usually a much less public "celebration" than the rites we're speaking of!

9. Back in the day, I heard this joke line used by both Wayne Rice (the godfather hero of all middle school ministry) and Jim Burns (now host of HomeWord). I don't know who originated it, but I've used it liberally for years.

10. For one example, see Rick Bundschuh's wonderful book about rites of passage for boys, *Passed Thru Fire: Bringing Boys into Meaningful Manhood* (Tyndale House, 2003).

11. It's rare to see this significant of a change in human physiology over such a short number of years. I'm actually quite surprised that I haven't seen scholarly articles connecting this to human evolution and speculating about the future. But, then, I don't read many scholarly articles! Oddly enough, G. Stanley Hall's 1904 description of adolescence as a time of "storm and stress" was predicated on a now-completely-debunked evolutionary theory spin-off that Hall held tightly to. The idea was that any species (humans included) should show, in their individual life-span development, the same patterns theorized to exist in the evolution of the entire species. With this foundation (which no scientists believe anymore, evolutionists or not, Christian or not), Hall suggested that a disruptive period ("storm and stress") *must* be present at this point in the human lifespan, since it is (he said) present in the evolutionary development of the human species. Ah, the implications of Stanley's folly, so many decades later!

12. I've often been surprised by how passionate Christians are about this issue. (Or maybe it would be more accurate to say they're dispassionate and ignore it, or they chalk it up to a purely cultural, nonphysiological shift that's bad and correctible.) Some time ago, I posted on my blog a book review of Scot McKnight's *The Real Mary* and merely ruminated about the intersection of God's selection of Mary and the older age of puberty in history. And the responses were shockingly angry! People suggested that since we don't really know when puberty occurred 2,000 years ago that maybe the age of puberty was actually younger than it's been in more recent decades. Well, we don't really know; but all indicators, including rites of passage that were tied to menarche (and

occurred in what we would now call mid-adolescence), give us a fairly good indication that puberty was occurring at least at 14.5 years, if not a bit older. Many speculate that it was likely 15 or 16 years old.

Chapter 4

1. "Checking for understanding" is a critical component of any teaching or parenting with middle schoolers. Because of their in-and-out-of-abstract-thinking minds, what they hear will often be very different than what you intend to communicate!

2. Piaget first proposed the theory in the early 1920s and then published a book that includes the theory in 1957, *Logic and Psychology*. I'm going to talk about only the last two stages in this book. But, for reference, the rest of them break down roughly like this:

   - Sensorimotor period (years 0–2)
   - Preoperational period (years 2–7)
   - Concrete operational period (years 7–11)
   - Formal operational period (years 11 and up)

   For a concise overview of these stages, and the theory as a whole, see the Wikipedia article on "The theory of cognitive development" at http://en.wikipedia.org/wiki/Theory_of_cognitive_development (accessed 3/13/09).

3. I remember doing a little firsthand testing for a research paper I wrote while I was in grad school, using some of the instruments Piaget used. I don't remember the whole thing, but I remember setting a few glasses of water in front of children and teens of various ages. In particular, one of the glasses was tall and thin, and another was short and wide. The short and wide glass had more water in it than the tall and thin glass; but the water level in the latter, due to its shape, was higher. When asked which glass had more water in it, the children universally choose the thin glass with the higher water level (but less actual content).

4. Among the other developmental theories based on the foundation established by Piaget are Lawrence Kohlberg's hotly contested theory of moral development and James Fowler's theory of faith development.

5. The general thinking regarding the reason for this delayed use of abstract thinking is that our culture doesn't expect teenagers to use abstract thinking, so they don't have much reason to exercise it. In fact, new research shows—this is alarming—that up to a full half of the *adult* population never fully engage in abstract thinking.

6. Two useless asides here: First, we never found the thumb tip. I've often morbidly wondered it if ended up as a green olive on someone's pizza. Second, this little skin graft surgery provided one of the most embarrassing moments of my life. I was stripped naked from the waist down

and lying on an outpatient table at a teaching hospital. All I had covering my crotch was a little towel. Just as the doctor started his prep work, a nurse walked in with what appeared to be about eight first-day *female* student nurses, all about my age. Just after they arrived, the towel interfered with the doctor's work, and he flicked it. I don't know if a puff of air came through at that moment or what, but the little towel lifted up like a helicopter and flew away. Now I was lying there, completely naked, in front of eight student nurses who were clearly the same age (about 18 or 19) as me. This would have been bad enough. But what made it horrifically worse was that they started giggling. It was one of those infectious giggles that starts with one person and becomes unavoidable as the others try not to giggle. Once they were all giggling, the nurse assisting in the surgery told the student nurse host to "get them out of here," and I was spared further horror.

7. Recent research has shown that the part of the human brain most responsible for many of these abstract functions—particularly functions such as hypothesizing, speculation, decision-making, and all things related to wisdom—is underdeveloped in teenagers and not fully formed (physiologically speaking) until the mid-twenties. There's still a good amount of debate on this, as the findings are so new; but the implications seem to be that teenagers gain this new abstract thinking ability at puberty. They wrestle with putting it into use not only because of inexperience, but also because their brains haven't finished developing yet. In other words, there's a biological explanation for why teenagers are so slow to "get" some of this stuff and why they're so notorious for poor decision-making, poor prioritization, and a general lack of wisdom. For more on this, read the excellent book *The Primal Teen: What the New Discoveries about the Teenage Brain Tell Us about Our Kids* by Barbara Strauch (Anchor, 2004). I'll discuss this more in a bit.

8. Psychological literature calls this an "imaginary audience."

9. The best book on this—a must-read for all parents—is one I mentioned in an earlier note: *The Primal Teen: What the New Discoveries about the Teenage Brain Tell Us about Our Kids* by Barbara Strauch (Anchor, 2004). This fascinating book covers this brain research in detail and lays out lots of the implications. An excellent overview of all of this brain stuff can also be found in this article: http://www.walrusmagazine.com/articles/2006.11-science-the-teenage-brain/1/ (accessed 3/13/09).

10. Giedd's findings are summarized in Barbara Strauch, *The Primal Teen: What the New Discoveries about the Teenage Brain Tell Us about Our Kids* (Anchor, 2004), 15-18.

11. This is an intentional overstatement, meant to make you think.

12. Here's an article that fleshes this need for sleep out a bit more: http://nymag.com/news/features/38951/ (accessed 3/13/09).

13. I wrote a blog post about this, which includes the car insurance ad referenced here: http://whyismarko.com/2007/teenage-brain-research-hits-the-streets/ (accessed 6/27/10).

14. Most notably, Dr. Robert Epstein, particularly in his book *Teen 2.0: Saving Our Children and Families from the Torment of Adolescence* (Quill Driver Books, 2010). Epstein's book was a game-changer for me, as were the subsequent conversations I've had with many other youth workers who have read the book, and the conversation I was able to have with the author. It's a thick and daunting book, but it's not difficult reading. I highly encourage you to read it, but be aware that you'll resonate with much of it, and—likely—experience extreme negative responses to other aspects of what Epstein suggests. Epstein's primary contention is that adolescence, as it's experienced in the United States, is harmful to teenagers and unnecessary. He suggests the delayed development of particular brain functions is a question of the chicken and the egg—which comes first? He believes the "new insights" on teenage brain development are an effect, not a cause, and that teen brains aren't fully developed because, culturally, we don't expect teenagers to use those parts of their brains. He believes adolescence is a false and purely cultural construct that has no basis in actual science. Interesting stuff, really.

Chapter 5

1. I'm not saying preteens have only four or five emotions at their emotional fingertips. It's a metaphor—stick with me.

2. I feel manlier just typing out this metaphor! Look at me, a guy who talks about tools!

3. If we're really honest with ourselves, we'll admit that this kind of harsh response is often because kids push our buttons with their strong emotions. Our responses become more about us than about them.

4. To gain a better understanding of how emotional development plays out for teenage girls, I'd suggest the following two excellent resources: *Odd Girl Out: The Hidden Culture of Aggression in Girls* by Rachel Simmons (Harvest Books, 2003) and *Teenage Girls: Exploring Issues Adolescent Girls Face and Strategies to Help Them* by Ginny Olson (Zondervan/Youth Specialties, 2006).

Chapter 6

1. Again, it's not that affinity plays no role in childhood friendships. It's just not the dominant theme. In young adolescence, as affinity becomes a pathway to figuring out one's identity, it begins to play a major role in friendship development—the major role.

2. This gender uniquenesses in friendship formation and culturally informed roles is discussed at length in a pair of excellent books: *Teenage Girls*

by Ginny Olson (Zondervan/Youth Specialties, 2006), and *Teenage Guys* by Steve Gerali (Zondervan/Youth Specialties, 2006). These books were written for church youth workers, but would be good reading for parents also.

3. Ken Rawson has written a helpful curriculum for middle school guys that addresses this very reality, called *Becoming a Young Man of God* (Zondervan/Youth Specialties, 2008). You might consider modifying it for use in devotions with your son.

4. For more on this, see David Livermore's *Cultural Intelligence: Improving Your CQ to Engage Our Multicultural World* (Baker Academic, 2009), particularly chapter 4 ("The Average American: Understanding Our Own Culture") and chapter 8 ("Why We Do What We Do: Cultural Values").

5. One of Youth Specialties' YS One Day team members brought these numbers to us as part of our content development a few years back. My reference searching seems to indicate that the numbers of 20,000 for females and 7,000 for guys (not the 4,000 I say in the text) comes from *The Female Brain* by Louann Brizendine (Broadway, 2007). This number seems hotly debated and disputed by researchers. But the observable reality is that *girls use more words than boys.*

Chapter 7

1. By the way, I'd also worked with the hotel to have all the pay-per-view movies blocked, as well as the hotel's free HBO channel. We encouraged the kids to stay off the phones, and we checked with the front desk to see if any of them were making lots of calls (then went to those rooms and talked to the kids). During our occasional "rounds," we listened for excessive noise (there were other guests in the hotel, of course!) and had a chat with those kids also, reapplying their bit of tape after we opened the door.

2. The other adolescent tasks are identity and affinity. I'll address this more in the chapter on culture (chapter 9).

3. See the Wikipedia article on individuation: http://en.wikipedia.org/wiki/Individuation (accessed 4/8/09).

4. We can add to the problem if we assume other parents don't have good motivation in how they address this process. Sure, there are parents who don't have healthy motivations, but the majority are erring because of wrongly applied good motivation.

5. I had to walk back to the movie entrance and call my dad. (Remember the days before cell phones?) He wasn't home, and my older sister agreed to pick us up. When I saw her car enter the parking lot, I decided to add a bit of levity to the awkward situation by jumping around the empty lot like a clown, shouting, "Over here! It's the one with no wheels!" But when the car pulled up, I saw that the driver was my understandably

frustrated father. We drove to my girlfriend's house in complete silence. And then, after we dropped her off, he said just one thing: "That's the most expensive date you'll ever go on."

6. The names (junior high, middle school) are somewhat meaningless these days, by the way, as population growth, shrinkage, and growth again have caused school systems to try all kinds of practical solutions, as well as some that are developmentally based.

Chapter 8

1. This reconsideration of one's faith often (although not always) happens at a subconscious, or at least a non-articulated, level.

2. Smith's work, based on a rigorous and fairly exhaustive longitudinal study with a large sample of American teenagers, was first summarized in his important book *Soul Searching: The Religious and Spiritual Lives of American Teenagers* (Oxford University Press, 2005). Smith found that "Moral Therapeutic Deism" was the dominant faith of teenagers in America. "Moral" = God wants me to be good, and the balance of good and bad in my life will determine something about the kind of life I get to have; "Therapeutic" = God is occasionally a cosmic butler, and can help me feel good; "Deism" = but, ultimately, God created the world and is now distant, not involved in my life. Smith also found that the number one reason for this being the dominant faith of American teenagers (including those active in churches) is that it's also the dominant faith of their parents.

3. This is a modification of "Bloom's Taxonomy," which I was first exposed to by Dr. Duane Elmer, at the Wheaton College Graduate School. I have modified the words, however. See more info on Bloom's Taxonomy here: http://en.wikipedia.org/wiki/Bloom%27s_taxonomy (accessed 3/13/09).

4. This holds true even with the trinity of the most interesting middle school subjects: sex, the end times, and "Will there be sex in the end times?"

5. Here's where this becomes a cycle, rather than the linear nature of Bloom's Taxonomy. Especially in spiritual growth (but also true in other kinds of learning), all that becomes a part of us through the "doing" phase informs our next pass(es) through the cycle.

6. See the whole story in John 20. By the way, I can't help noticing that Thomas's response has all the emotional and offensive exaggeration we might expect from a middle schooler (not that he was one). It was pretty crass for him to say he'd only believe Jesus were alive if he had the chance to insert his hand in the gory, gaping wound in Jesus' side!

Chapter 9

1. I compiled most of this list from my own experience, and the experience of my previous co-author, Scott Rubin. But we got some additional help

from respondents to my blog: http://whyismarko.com/2008/things-that-didnt-exist-when-we-were-in-middle-school/ (accessed 6/27/10).

2. Kara Powell and Brad Griffin's "bonus chapter" at the end of this book focuses on the subject of what's changed for middle school girls. Make sure you check it out!

3. This is the primary premise of my book *Youth Ministry 3.0: A Manifesto of Where We've Been, Where We Are, and Where We Need to Go* (Zondervan/Youth Specialties, 2008). It would be good supplemental reading to this youth culture section.

4. My contention in *Youth Ministry 3.0*, which I won't go into in this book, is that youth ministry did a good job of responding to these shifts in the first and second epochs. Early youth workers, in the '50s and '60s, created approaches to youth ministry that were a response to this new culture and responsive to the identity priority in culture. In the late '60s and early '70s, a new kind of youth ministry sprang up that was responsive to the shift toward autonomy, and the modern "youth group" was formed. The challenge we're facing now is that most of our youth ministries are using models and assumptions and values that are responsive to this second epoch when our kids are part of the third wave of youth culture (with a priority on affinity or belonging).

5. Chap Clark writes extensively about this "going underground" aspect of youth culture in his excellent book *Hurt: Inside the World of Today's Teenagers* (Baker Academic, 2004).

6. Dictionary.com Unabridged (v 1.1). Random House, Inc., http://dictionary.reference.com/browse/culture (accessed 3/13/09).

7. M. T. Anderson has written a fascinating piece of young adult fiction called *Feed* (Candlewick, 2004). It tells the futuristic story of teen drama (budding romance, shifting friendships, wrestling with adolescent tasks). But the significant feature of this "brave new world" is the wireless "feed" that's installed in the brains of all teenagers (and most adults), which allows for a constant flow of marketing, video programming, human interaction (think text messaging via brain waves), and other functions. The feed is wired into the brain, so if the characters notice someone's jeans, they start receiving an onslaught of marketing in their minds about sales on jeans. It's nuts. But the most disconcerting thing about the book is that it doesn't seem quite far-fetched enough. Recommended reading – it might even be interesting to read with your teen (though I wouldn't suggest it for a teen under 13), and talk about how to exercise discernment through the onslaught of information and marketing constantly bombarding us.

8. This sedentary lifestyle (combined with fatty, starch- and sugar-filled diets) is the leading cause in the massive rise of obesity in children and teenagers.

9. Of course, like much of this chapter, this is a generalization. There are lots of kids who spend all of their free time at the skateboard park or living some other physical lifestyle.

Chapter 10

1. Incidentally, I was with a group of ninth-grade boys recently, standing on the curb of a busy street, waiting to cross. One of them said, "Let's play *Frogger!*" I responded with shock, "What!?" They thought I'd never heard of *Frogger,* which was funny in and of itself since the game was popular before they were even born. When they tried to explain the video game, I cut them off, telling them I was very clear about what that game was. They went on to explain that they wanted to play a live version, where they run out into traffic, dodging the cars. I looked at them with horror: *Were they kidding?* No, it was clear they were not. Ah, the judgment skills of young teens. It's a wonder any of them survive. Needless to say, I did not allow the live version of *Frogger* on my watch.

2. I asked for help with this metaphor on my blog, and Jose Samuel Merida suggested the color change between adjacent colors in a rainbow. I'm not using the rainbow part of his metaphorical suggestion, but the color blend really seemed to work for me.

Bonus Chapter

1. Portions of this chapter were modified from articles titled "New Twists on Not-So-New Issues for Girls," "See Jane Deal with Her Body," and "See Jane Navigate Technology," all authored by Kara Powell and Brad Griffin and available at www.fulleryouthinstitute.org.

2. Harris Interactive, "A Generation Unplugged" Research Report (September 12, 2008), http://www.ctia.org/advocacy/research/index.cfm/AID/11483 (accessed 3/13/09).

3. American Psychological Association (APA), Task Force on the Sexualization of Girls, *Report of the APA Task Force on the Sexualization of Girls* (2007), 3, http://www.apa.org/pi/wpo/sexualizationrep.pdf (accessed 3/13/09).

4. Ibid., 16. For more information, check out the "2005 Age Distribution: Cosmetic Patients (18 or Younger)" PDF available at http://www.plasticsurgery.org/Media/Statistics/2005_Statistics.html (accessed 3/13/09).

5. The Tucker Center for Research on Girls & Women in Sport, University of Minnesota, Minneapolis, MN, "Developing Physically Active Girls: An Evidence-Based Multidisciplinary Approach" (2007), http://cehd.umn.edu/TuckerCenter/projects/TCRR/executive-summary.html (accessed 3/13/09).

6. Lan Nguyen Chaplin and Deborah Roedder John, "Growing Up in a Material World: Age Differences in Materialism in Children and Adolescents," *Journal of Consumer Research* 34 (Dec. 2007).

7. Dorothy Espelage, professor of educational psychology at the University of Illinois, Urbana-Champaign, quoted in Vanessa O'Connell, "Fashion Bullies Attack—In Middle School" *Wall Street Journal,* October 25, 2007, D1.

8. *Report of the APA Task Force on the Sexualization of Girls,* 41.

About the Author

Mark Oestreicher is a 30-year middle school ministry veteran who is widely known as one of the leading voices in youth ministry. Oestreicher's particular passion and calling is with young teens. After serving in multiple churches as a junior high or middle school pastor, Marko (as he's known to friends and youth workers) spent eleven years at Youth Specialties, the leading publisher and training event provider for church-based youth workers. During the last eight years of his time with Youth Specialties, Marko was the president. He also served for four years on the leadership team of Zondervan after Zondervan acquired YS in 2006.

Marko is the author of more than 50 books, many of which are for or about middle school ministry, or for middle schoolers themselves. His last two books, *Youth Ministry 3.0* and *Middle School Ministry* (coauthored with Scott Rubin), have been much talked about and reviewed, and read by thousands of youth workers. For your young teen, Marko's last series of books was the six-book Middle School Survival Series (*My Faith, My Family, My Friends, My School, My Changes,* and *My Future*), each coauthored with either Kurt Johnston or Scott Rubin. Many of the ideas in the book you're holding are covered, in a young-teen-appropriate way, in the book *My Changes.* (Having your young teen read that book while you read this one could create some interesting conversations!)

These days, Marko is "having a blast" (he says) leading The Youth Cartel, an organization that provides services for church youth workers and organizations trying to connect with teenagers and youth workers. Marko's blog, www.whyismarko.com, has about 2,000 daily readers and was recently named the #2 youth ministry blog.

Marko is an active volunteer leader in his church, where he occasionally preaches, coaches a few of the pastors, and leads a middle school boys small group. Marko's been married to Jeannie for 25 years and has two children, Liesl (17) and Max (13). Marko and his family live in La Mesa, California, just east of San Diego.

Marko's blog: www.whyismarko.com

Marko's Web site: www.theyouthcartel.com

Marko invites you to contact him via the contact page of his Web site if you have any questions.

My Changes

Mark Oestreicher and Scott Rubin

In *My Changes*, a book written for young teens, they'll discover the reasons behind a lot of their changes, and get tips on how to survive all of them. They will find valuable insights on changes happening in their body, their brain and thoughts, their identity, their emotions, their gender, and more.

After reading *My Changes* and other books in the Middle School Survival Series, they'll be ready to take on the rest of middle school with the confidence and knowledge they'll need to survive (and thrive) as a young teen.

Available in stores and online!

THE YOUTH CARTEL

instigating a revolution in youth ministry

The Youth Cartel's mission is to encourage and challenge adults who minister to youth through holistic professional coaching, strategic consulting, transformational events, and inventive resource development that advance youth ministry in new ways.

While The Youth Cartel exists to serve church youth workers and organizations that want to reach youth workers, we have two weekly emails that could be very helpful to parents.

YouTube You Can Use
A free weekly discussion guide based on a popular viral video. This would make an easy and fun family devotion. http://theyouthcartel.com/newsletter

Cartel Culture
This weekly resource helps adults stay current on matters of youth culture and the church. Great for parents who want to stay abreast of articles, research and ideas impacting teenagers. http://theyouthcartel.com/newsletter

visit theyouthcartel.com

Share Your Thoughts

With the Author: Your comments will be forwarded to the author when you send them to *zauthor@zondervan.com*.

With Zondervan: Submit your review of this book by writing to *zreview@zondervan.com*.

Free Online Resources at
www.zondervan.com

Zondervan AuthorTracker: Be notified whenever your favorite authors publish new books, go on tour, or post an update about what's happening in their lives at www.zondervan.com/authortracker.

Daily Bible Verses and Devotions: Enrich your life with daily Bible verses or devotions that help you start every morning focused on God. Visit www.zondervan.com/newsletters.

Free Email Publications: Sign up for newsletters on Christian living, academic resources, church ministry, fiction, children's resources, and more. Visit www.zondervan.com/newsletters.

Zondervan Bible Search: Find and compare Bible passages in a variety of translations at www.zondervanbiblesearch.com.

Other Benefits: Register yourself to receive online benefits like coupons and special offers, or to participate in research.